SAVING YOUR FUTURE

Basic Principles of Building a
Financial Foundation

WORLD SYSTEM BUILDER

ACKNOWLEDGMENTS

Teamwork is dreamwork. This project is a collaborative effort of many people.

We are indebted to the home office, both in the U.S. and Canada, for their expertise.

Angelo Gurrieri, Victor Salvador, Alicia Nguyen, and Tuan Le were instrumental for their support and advice.

A special thanks to Nick Nguyen, Tammy Luong, and Tina Quach for their work in editing and designing the book.

Xuan Nguyen, together with input from Zhong Shi, Xiao Lin, and Carl Meldrum, were key contributors who made this book possible.

For the team and by the team, this book is dedicated to all the hard working men and women who are committed to making a difference for families and building a strong financial foundation for their future.

PRESS

www.worldsystembuilder.com

TABLE OF CONTENTS

INTRODUCTION

FINANCIAL FOUNDATION

THE X-CURVE

INSURANCE

INVESTMENT

RETIREMENT

OTHER SOLUTIONS

CONCLUSION

DISCLAIMER

This book is written for both the U.S. and Canada. While many similarities exist between the two countries' financial and economic systems, there are some differences in regards to certain products and services. However, the key important financial concepts of how money works are the same.

The purpose of this book is to provide a general understanding about financial concepts and information. It's not intended to give advice on tax, insurance, investment, or any product and service. Since each of us has our own unique situations, you should have all the appropriate information to understand and make the right decision to fit with your needs and your financial goals. We hope that you will succeed in building your financial future.

Neither the author nor any other person associated with this book may be held liable for any damages that may result from the contents of this book.

No book can be used as a substitute for professional, personalized advice. Readers are encouraged to seek financial advice from qualified professionals, including licensed investment advisors, stockbrokers, accountants, insurance agents, attorneys, CPAs, and other qualified individuals.

World System Builder is a financial services marketing organization that is associated with World Financial Group, Inc. World Financial Group, Inc. (WFG) is a financial services marketing company whose affiliates offer a broad array of financial products and services. Insurance products offered through World Financial Group Insurance Agency, Inc. (WFGIA), World Financial Group Insurance Agency of Hawaii, Inc., World Financial Group Insurance Agency of Massachusetts, Inc., World Financial Group Insurance Agency of Wyoming, Inc., World Financial Insurance Agency, Inc. and/or WFG Insurance Agency of Puerto Rico, Inc. Securities and Investment Advisory Services offered through Transamerica Financial Advisors, Inc. (TFA), Transamerica Financial Group Division - Member FINRA, SIPC, and Registered Investment Advisor. Non-Securities products and services are not offered through TFA. Only WFG associates who are Registered Representatives and/or Investment Advisor Representatives of Transamerica Financial Advisors, Inc. can offer investment products and/or investment advisory services. WFG, WFGIA and TFA are affiliated companies. World System Builder and Transamerica Financial Advisors, Inc. Transamerica Financial Group Division are not affiliated. World System Builder Headquarters: 2099 Gold Street, Suite 100, Alviso, CA 95002. Phone: 408.941.1838.

The views and opinions expressed thereon are those of the author, and not necessarily those of World Financial Group, Inc. Neither World Financial Group, nor its licensed associates offer tax and legal advice. All mathematical examples presented are hypothetical and are for illustrative purposes only. They are not intended to represent any specific product. Examples do not consider any cost associated with a product.

saving

your

future

INTRODUCTION

According to recent surveys, North Americans are facing serious financial challenges.

In Canada:

✦ 35% of Canadians do not have any savings or investments.

✦ Only 27% of private sector workers have an employer-funded pension plan.

✦ The average savings in Registered Retirement Savings Plans (RRSP) is only $55,000.*

The U.S. picture is even gloomier.

✦ 33%, or more than 77 million, of Americans don't pay their bills on time.

✦ 39% carry credit card debt from month to month.

✦ Only 59% of adults say they have savings.

✦ Worse, more than half now think it's acceptable to default on their mortgage if they can't afford to pay it.**

Most of us don't wait to become a statistic to know that we're in trouble. These problems are all around us. They happen to our own family and our friends' families.

It's ironic that we live in one of the wealthiest countries in the world, but we always have money problems. We can work hard all our lives but retire poor. We do so much to raise our kids just to see them finish college with a lot of debt. Debt becomes a way of life.

We don't have much, and we don't know much. Nobody teaches us how to manage our money in school. Financial issues are not often discussed, and financial products not always explained. Most people have trouble balancing their own checkbook and reading a financial statement. We use credit cards every day and don't always understand all the hidden charges. We buy insurance policies and stick them in a file cabinet. We contribute to our 401k or RRSP and hope someone will take care of it. We all want to have a comfortable retirement, but few have a plan. We may be active spenders but passive savers.

It's possible that we don't know what we don't know. Even though the financial industry is one of the largest industries in the world, and even though we are flooded with financial news, channels, and websites, financial literacy is as murky as ever.

There is a jungle of complex rules and regulations for the thousands of stocks, bonds, funds, savings plans, credit cards, and loans out there.

We need to change, and the task won't be easy. But we need understanding first. The old days of passive dependence have to end. A new era of proactivism and financial freedom must begin.

For this book, we want to explain finance as how a friend would talk to another friend. We want to make it simple enough, using common language for common people. We don't intend to get into a lot of detail but are more focused on the fundamentals of how money works. We try to use simple examples and common assumptions.

The best we can hope for is to get your attention and interest into financial matters and for you to obtain some basics of how money works. It's the first step toward your financial future. Like many of us, once you enter the gate of financial knowledge, you'll discover that it's doable to understand, plan, and build a financial foundation for your family.

Remember: There is nobody more interested in your financial future than you are, definitely not the government or your employer. It's your responsibility to learn the simple rules of how money works. Understanding how money works is part of taking care of your family. You can do it. You can control your future.

*http://abclifeliteracy.ca/mm/financial-literacy-facts
**http://www.creditcards.com/credit-card-news/consumer-financial-literacy-survey-1276.php

THE NEW WORLD

Turbulence marked the new millennium.

As the last hours counted down to the year 2000, the fear of the Y2K computer bug threatened to wreck world order into cyber chaos.

By mid-March of that year, the dot.com bubble burst, sending the stock market into freefall.

One year later, the September 11th tragedy ushered in a new reality of uncertainty and insecurity.

Then in 2008 the world experienced another financial crisis. The U.S. economy dragged under the Great Recession.

The first decade of the new millennium was a lost decade for so many families. They suffered huge losses in home values, savings, retirement accounts, and worst of all their employment. A massive number of people went into bankruptcy and foreclosure. Millions gave up hope looking for work.

While these turbulent times may have been more pronounced in the U.S. than in Canada, average Canadians were not immune to the impact of declining markets and a less certain future.

Although the U.S. economy is now recovering, the aftermath carries on.

Today, there are 76 million Baby Boomers, people born between 1946 to 1964. Every day, 10,000 of them turn 65. Many of them were hit hard by the financial crisis. Many more struggle to survive because they did not prepare for retirement.

Generation X, born between 1965 to 1980, are middle-aged adults. They are worried about keeping their jobs and paying growing bills. Many of them are sandwiched between the burden of taking care of their own family and helping their parents.

Millennials, those born after 1980, are facing even bigger hurdles with the new economy. As the labor market becomes global, companies are increasingly sending their operations overseas where labor costs are lower. In addition, more jobs are being replaced due to advances in software and automation. Technology and smart machines change so fast that workers' skills may not be able to keep pace.*

Many people will be left behind or will have to settle for lower skilled jobs and temporary employment.

http://www.pewsocialtrends.org/2014/03/07/millennials-in-adulthood/sdt-next-america-03-07-2014-0-06

THE NEW AWAKENING

After World War II, the second half of the last millennium presented a comfortable way of life. Most people grew up thinking: If they could go to a good college, get a good degree, and find a good job, then when they retire, their union, their company, or the government would take care of them. Saving was not a priority.

Toward the 1980's and 90's, money became more accessible through easier loans and credit cards. Spend now and pay later was the mantra. Consumer debt soared. Living with debt became the new norm. From college until old age, many people went through a lifetime of debt beginning with student loans and on to credit cards, car loans, mortgages, etc.

Perhaps the only good thing to come out of the last financial crisis is that more and more people are starting to pay attention to their personal finances. They want to understand how money works and rebuild their financial foundation.

SELF SECURITY

The traditional pillars of retirement are now in doubt.

Personal Savings

38 million Americans are currently living paycheck to paycheck.*

Canada is not doing better. 30% percent of Canadians can't handle more than $500 of unexpected expenses without going into debt, and an additional 28% can't handle more than $2000.**

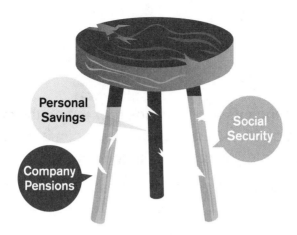

Company Pensions

The good old days of pensions are disappearing in North America. In the U.S., companies now offer 401ks, and few match contributions. In Canada, companies have been moving away from Defined Benefit Plans that provide a known retirement amount to Defined Contribution Plans that leave the investment risks with the worker.

Government Programs:
Social Security and Canada Pension Plan

In the 1940s, for every retiree there were over 40 American workers contributing to Social Security. Today this number has shrunk to roughly 3 per retiree.*** This imbalance will put increasing pressure on the government's ability to sustain Social Security and provide benefits to seniors who are living longer and require more support.

In Canada, there are similar pressures on the Canada Pension Plan (CPP) caused by an aging population that is living longer. As of January 2015, if you were to qualify for the maximum monthly retirement pension at age 65, it would be $1,065 per month.**** Is this enough to provide you with the secure retirement that you desire?

More than ever, people need to change their thinking from Social Security to Self Security. You must fund your own retirement. You can't depend on unions, your employer, or the government. You must take charge of your financial future and develop new financial habits.

- ✦ **Make Money**
- ✦ **Save Money**
- ✦ **Grow Money**
- ✦ **Protect Money**

Financial concepts and solutions may not be the most exciting subject. But with discipline and patience, you can learn and understand the fundamentals. And you can build a good financial foundation.

Financial independence is not a dream. It is a priority. Take control of your future.

*http://money.cnn.com/2014/04/25/news/economy/middle-class-paycheck
**http://www.benefitscanada.com/news/canadians-say-their-savings-habits-are-poor-55872
***http://mercatus.org/publication/how-many-workers-support-one-social-security-retiree
****http://www.benefitscanada.com/pensions/db/cpp-benefits-rising-in-2015-60918

FINANCIAL FOUNDATION

Like building a house, you should start with a solid financial foundation and build it from the ground up.

| INVESTMENT |
| EMERGENCY FUND |
| DEBT MANAGEMENT |
| PROTECTION |

First, you should have proper protection in the event of disability, health problems, or premature death.

You should reduce your liability and get out of debt.

You should set aside 3 to 6 months of your income to deal with sudden changes in your job or business or to pay for unforeseen accidents or repairs.

And you should save and invest for the long run.

All these tasks should be done as soon as possible.

As a priority, you should consider protection first. Why? If you try to save a few hundred dollars a month but have no insurance, when you get sick, disabled, or die suddenly, this savings won't last very long.

Likewise, if you have an emergency, but your money is tied up in some investment, how would you deal with sudden unexpected expenses? You may have to get into more debt.

A strong foundation will build a sturdier, more enduring financial house. Otherwise, it won't remain standing when the storms, tornadoes, and earthquakes strike. Thus, the 4 financial foundation layers will build solid ground for your financial future.

UNDERSTAND HOW MONEY WORKS
The Wealth Formula

Money doesn't grow on trees. You must work for it. If you want to build wealth, there is a formula for you to build on:

$$\begin{array}{r} \text{MONEY} \\ + \text{ TIME} \\ +/- \text{ RATE OF RETURN} \\ - \text{ INFLATION} \\ - \text{ TAX} \\ \hline = \text{WEALTH} \end{array}$$

This is a concept/goal developed by World Financial Group (WFG) for illustrative purposes only. In no way does this statement offer, guarantee or otherwise imply any financial gain or reward as a result of joining WFG. The term "wealth" is subjective and must be defined on an individual basis.

MONEY TALK

Where is the money? A good number of people always seem to have money problems. Most of the time, they're short on funds. Warren Buffet advises, "Don't save what is left after spending; spend what is left after saving."

Pay Yourself First

Set aside 5 to 10% of your income to save for the future. If possible, save 15% or more. Treat it like a bill that you must pay, and pay it first. That's your "family financial bill". Doesn't it make sense to pay your family first before paying other people's bills? Your cable TV bill is not more important than your family's financial well-being.

Buy Only What You Need

Spending money is a way of life for many people. Shopping becomes a habit. It can become an addiction.

Finding bargains and buying on-sale items don't always mean that you're saving. It could be that you're buying things you don't necessarily need.

Know the difference between what you really need and what you want. When a person says they "need" new shoes, is it truly essential or simply a desire? How many people intend to buy a Toyota but drive home with a Lexus?

Small Changes, Big Money

Spending is a habit, so is saving. What if you could make small changes to your spending habits and start saving $10 a day? That's $300 per month.

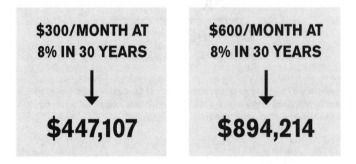

These are sizeable amounts for your retirement. Can you cut down on some personal luxuries now to reap greater benefits in the future? Things like soda, lattes, bottled water, cigarettes, cable TV, high-end gadgets, new phones, shopping, fancy cars, eating out, partying?

It's not what you earn that counts. It's what you keep. A common characteristic among wealthy people is that they're very conscientious about their spending.

TIME

Time is money.

The sooner you save, the better for your future. Let's take a look at the examples on the next page.

Procrastination is the enemy of saving. When many people are young, they think they have a lot of time to save. Then they get married, have kids, and buy a house. With a mortgage and new expenses, money becomes tight. They tell themselves they will start saving later.

As they enter mid life, their children go to college, and tuition takes a big bite out of their budget. Soon they will join the majority of people approaching retirement with little to no savings. They know they must save, but now they say it's too late.

Many wonder: What if they had just put aside $100 or $200 a month when they were young? They could have accumulated significant assets today.

Don't wait. Start to save as much as you can, as soon as you can.

GET RICH SLOWLY

A solid foundation takes time to build. Trees don't grow big overnight.

Avoid get-rich-quick impulses. Hot stocks and rising real estate markets can sound appealing. But one wrong pick can set you back big time from your savings goal.

Investing is not gambling. You must understand how money works, have a plan, and stay disciplined with your action plan until you reach your goal.

SAVE EARLY

**Mr. Start Early saves $3,600 per year for 7 years
in a 8% tax-deferred account.**

**Mr. Wait Longer starts saving $3,600 per year for 17 years
in a 8% tax-deferred account, 7 years later than Mr. Start Early.**

For illustration purposes only.

	MR. START EARLY			MR. WAIT LONGER	
Age	Yearly Contribution	Total Accumulation	Age	Yearly Contribution	Total Accumulation
25	$3600	$3,888	25	$ -	0
26	$3600	$8,087	26	$ -	0
27	$3600	$12,622	27	$ -	0
28	$3600	$17,520	28	$ -	0
29	$3600	$22,809	29	$ -	0
30	$3600	$28,522	30	$ -	0
31	$3600	$34,692	31	$ -	0
32	$ -	$37,467	32	$3600	$3,888
33	$ -	$40,465	33	$3600	$8,087
34	$ -	$43,702	34	$3600	$12,622
35	$ -	$47,198	35	$3600	$17,520
36	$ -	$50,974	36	$3600	$22,809
37	$ -	$55,052	37	$3600	$28,522
38	$ -	$59,456	38	$3600	$34,692
39	$ -	$64,212	39	$3600	$41,355
40	$ -	$69,349	40	$3600	$48,552
41	$ -	$74,897	41	$3600	$56,324
42	$ -	$80,889	42	$3600	$64,718
43	$ -	$87,360	43	$3600	$73,783
44	$ -	$94,349	44	$3600	$83,574
45	$ -	$101,897	45	$3600	$94,148
46	$ -	$110,048	46	$3600	$105,567
47	$ -	$118,852	47	$3600	$117,901
48	$ -	$128,361	48	$3600	$131,221

Total Contribution	Total Contribution
$25,200	**$61,200**

RATE OF RETURN
The Magic of Compound Interest

One of the most important discoveries in finance is the Rule of 72.* It shows you how to calculate the effect of compound interest with a very simple formula.

Take 72 and divide it by the rate of return. The answer is the number of years it takes to double your money.

$$\frac{72}{\text{Rate of Return}} = \text{years to double your money}$$

For example: With 4% interest

$$\frac{72}{4} = \text{18 years to double your money}$$

THE RULE OF 72

72 / 4 = 18		72 / 8 = 9		72 / 12 = 6	
Money doubles every 18 years		Money doubles every 9 years		Money doubles every 6 years	
Age	4%	Age	8%	Age	12%
29	$10,000	29	$10,000	29	$10,000
				35	$20,000
		38	$20,000	41	$40,000
47	$20,000	47	$40,000	47	$80,000
				53	$160,000
		56	$80,000	59	$320,000
65	$40,000	65	$160,000	65	$640,000

The difference between $10,000 at 4% versus 12% is $600,000. $600,000 is equal to 20 years salary of someone who earns $30,000 annually.

The Rule of 72 unveils the powerful impact of compound interest on money. It also reveals 2 types of people.

+ People who don't understand how money works–they end up working for money.

+ People who understand how money works–they let money work for them.

Wealthy people tend to spend time learning and understanding how money works. They look for advice and solutions to get better returns for their money.

A lot of poor people lack knowledge about personal finance. Some don't care to understand. Many have no plan and little savings. What savings they have are usually put into accounts with a low rate of return. Their money doesn't work for them.

Compound interest works both ways. It can make you, and it can break you. If you owe money, the compound interest on your debt can ruin you. As a result, many people keep paying the bill with high interest. Despite numerous payments, the balance of the bill barely goes down because high interest on the balance continues to compound. Sometimes, it feels as if it's impossible to pay the balance off.

The Rule of 72 is a mathematical concept that approximates the number of years it will take to double the principal at a constant rate of return. The performance of investments fluctuates over time and, as a result, the actual time it will take an investment to double in value cannot be predicated with any certainty. Additionally, there are no guarantees that any investment or savings program can outpace inflation. This is a hypothetical example and is not intended to represent a real investment. Both the principal and returns of investments vary over time. Seeking higher rates of return involves greater risk.

SIMPLE INTEREST vs COMPOUND INTEREST

Let's take an example of Mr. A putting $10,000 in a savings vehicle with 8% simple interest and Mr. B putting $10,000 in another savings vehicle with 8% compound interest annually.

Mr. A – Simple Interest

	Total
Year 1: $10,000 x 8% = $800	$10,800
Year 2: $10,000 x 8% = $800	$11,600
Year 3: $10,000 x 8% = $800	$12,400
Year 10: ⟶	**$18,000**

With simple interest, Mr. A earns $800 every year or $18,000 over 10 years.

Mr. B – Compound Interest

Total

Year 1: $10,000 x 8% = $800 $800 + $10,000 = $10,800

Year 2: $10,800 x 8% = $864 $864 + $10,800 = $11,664

Year 3: $11,664 x 8% = $933 $933 + $11,664 = $12,597

Year 10: ⟶   = **$21,589**

With compound interest, the savings vehicle of Mr. B gives him 8% on combined principal plus interest for the next year's calculation. When you see the difference between simple and compound interest, you now understand how powerful it can be.

THE REAL RATE OF RETURN

When you save or invest, it's important to have a good rate of return. But what's the real rate of return? In other words, what do you really get?

Example 1:		**Example 2:**	
If you save	$100.00	If you save	$100.00
at 3% interest	+ 3.00	At 5% interest	+ 5.00
Pay tax at 25%	- .75	Pay Tax at 25%	- 1.25
(Combined Fed & State)	———	(Combined Fed & State)	———
Net after Tax	$102.25	Net after tax	$103.75
Inflation at 3.5%	- 3.50	Inflation at 3.5%	- 3.50
Actual return	$98.75	Actual return	$100.25
(After tax and inflation)		(After tax and inflation)	

You Lose! (Example 1)

You must get about 5% or more in interest to beat taxes and inflation. (Example 2)

INFLATION:
The Silent Killer

Inflation is the rise in prices of goods and services over time.

When prices increase, your purchasing power decreases. For example, if the inflation rate is 3.5%, your $100 today will only be worth $96.50 next year.

Inflation happens when a country prints more money than it earns. The result is everybody will lose some value of their money. Some refer to inflation as a hidden tax.

Inflation is a major factor to consider when you build up your financial future. For instance, if you put your money in an account with a zero rate of return, its value will certainly decline in the long run.

In the last 100 years from 1914 to 2014, the U.S. inflation rate averaged 3.32%.* Let's take a look at the prices of some basic items over time.**

Average Cost of Living:

	The 70s	The 90s	2013
New Home	$23,450	$123,000	$289,500
New Car	$3,400	$16,950	$31,352
Loaf of Bread	25 cents	70 cents	$1.98
Wages	$9,400	$28,960	$44,321

What will your $100 do in the next 20 years? Assuming the inflation rate is 3%:

TODAY'S $100

Years From Now	Purchasing Power Decrease	Increased Inflation Amount to Equal $100
5	$86	$116
10	$74	$134
15	$64	$156
20	$55	$181

Say you plan to retire with $4,000 income per month in today's value. 20 years later, at a 3% inflation rate, you will need to have $7,224 per month to maintain the same purchasing power. Are you prepared for it? Do you think that you should save more and spend less?

*http://www.tradingeconomics.com/united-states/inflation-cpi
**http://www.thepeoplehistory.com

TAXES

Benjamin Franklin said that nothing is certain in this world except for death and taxes.

You make money. They tax you.

You spend money. They tax you.

You save money. They tax you.

You die. They still tax you.

From sales tax to income tax to property tax to estate tax and every other tax, anywhere you turn, the tax collectors await.

One bit of good news is that the highest current U.S. federal income tax rate is rather low compared with the past. It was over 90% during President Kennedy's time and 70% at the beginning of the Reagan era. Today, the top tax bracket is lower. But if you add state income tax, the total may be higher. For current tax rates, please visit *www.irs.gov*.

HISTORY OF INCOME TAX RATES (1913 TO 2015)*

Year	Top Bracket Rate	Comment
1913	7%	First permanent income tax
1917	67%	World War I financing
1932	63%	Depression era
1941	81%	World War II
1944	94%	Individual Income Tax Act of 1944
1964	77%	Tax reduction during Vietnam war
1981	70%	Reagan era tax cuts
1988	28%	Reagan era tax cuts
1991	31%	Omnibus Budget Reconciliation Act of 1990
2003	35%	Bush tax cuts
2013 – Present	39.6%	American Taxpayer Relief Act of 2012

*http://www.taxfoundation.org

While Canadians have different tax brackets and rates and some differences in the taxes they pay such as GST/HST, the ultimate impact and effect of taxes are the same. It leaves less money in your pocket. For current Canadian tax rates, please visit: *http://www.cra-arc.gc.ca/tx/ndvdls/ fq/txrts-eng.html*.

A TAXING ISSUE

Taxes take a big chunk of your money. Any saving and investment strategy must consider the tax impact on it. What is your current tax rate? What will the tax rate be in the future? Will taxes rise or fall?

Let's look at the challenges ahead.

1. The Shrinking Tax Base

As mentioned, since 1945 when Social Security began, workers per retiree shrank from over 40 to about 3 today. And the number continues to decline due to the aging demographics of the U.S. and Canada. Governments will have a hard time sustaining the existing systems of Social Security, the Canadian Pension Plan, and the general benefits that seniors receive today.

2. Mounting Debts

As of January 2015, the U.S. debt stands at $18 trillion—a burden of $56,500 per citizen. It was just $13 trillion 4 years ago. Canada's debt is C$692.4 billion, an average burden of C$19,590 per citizen.[**]

Guess who is going to pay for this debt? Our future generations. The government borrows most of it through public debt, which it owes to individuals, businesses, and foreign governments who bought Treasury bills, notes, and bonds. Foreign investors hold the largest share of the U.S. national debt. China and Japan top the list, holding more than $1 trillion each in IOUs.[***]

As the tax base for workers per retiree is shrinking, the costs to provide retirement benefits, Medicare, defense, and infrastructure continue to rise. The government will have to choose between cutting down the budget or raising taxes. Many people believe taxes may have to go up in the future. What do you think?

*http://www.usdebtclock.org
**http://www.nationaldebtclocks.org
***http://www.washingtonpost.com/blogs/worldviews/wp/2013/10/10/this-surprising-chart-shows-which-countries-own-the-most-u-s-debt

CAPITAL GAINS TAX

Almost everything you own and use for personal or investment purposes is a capital asset, like your home, stocks, and bonds. So when you sell capital assets, the difference between the amount you sold it for and your basis, which is usually what you paid for it, is a capital gain or capital loss.

Capital gains on assets held for less than one year is a short-term gain and usually taxed at ordinary income tax rates.

TAX NOW–TAX LATER–TAX ADVANTAGED

Where does your money go? Let's take a look at the following tax treatment on different types of investment accounts.

In the U.S.

Where Do You Put Your Money?

Tax Now	Tax Later	Tax Advantaged
CHECKING	401k/403(b)	ROTH-IRA
SAVINGS	IRA/SEP-IRA	529 COLLEGE SAVINGS
CD	ANNUITY	MUNICIPAL BOND
STOCK	PENSION	HEALTH SAVING
MUTUAL FUND		ACCOUNT (HSA)
		LIFE INSURANCE
		LONG TERM CARE BENEFIT

In Canada

Where Do You Put Your Money?

Tax Now	Tax Later	Tax Advantaged
CHEQUEING	RRSP/RRIF	TFSA
SAVINGS	LIRA/LIF	LIFE INSURANCE BENEFIT
GIC	RESP	INDIVIDUAL CRITICAL
STOCK	ANNUITY	ILLNESS AND DISABILITY
MUTUAL FUND	PENSION	INSURANCE
BOND	CPP	HEALTH INSURANCE
INTEREST INCOME	OAS	PRIMARY RESIDENCE
NON-REGISTERED	RDSP	
INVESTMENTS		

TAX NOW

Tax now means that any earnings from these accounts must pay tax for that year. For example, you must report and pay tax on earnings from savings accounts, Certificates of Deposit (CDs), dividends from stocks, mutual funds, and money market funds. In Canada, Guaranteed Investment Certificates (GICs), Term Deposits, and any investment or savings generally held in a non-registered plan would fall into this category.

TAX LATER

Tax later means the money you put in is pre-tax. Pre-tax money deposited in an account is money that you have not yet paid income tax on. But you'll definitely be paying tax later when you withdraw it. These accounts are also called "tax deferred". In the U.S., tax-deferred accounts commonly take the form of IRAs, 401ks, and 403(b)s. In Canada, Registered Retirement Savings Plans (RRSPs), Registered Educational Savings Plans (RESPs), and Registered Disability Savings Plans (RDSPs) are popular tax-deferred vehicles.

In the U.S., when you begin to take your money out after 59½, you'll be taxed at ordinary income tax rates. But if you take money out before 59½, you will get a 10% penalty (with few exceptions) in addition to taxes. Also, you can't keep money there forever. You must start withdrawing it when you reach 70½ or pay a 50% penalty.

Most tax later accounts are designed this way. However, some "Tax Later" accounts are tax deferred but not tax deductible. For example, the money you put into a non-qualified annuity or a non-deductible IRA is after-tax money, which is non-deductible. The tax only applies to the gain at withdrawal, which has been tax deferred.

Canadian RRSP rules are different from those in the U.S. However, the basic functioning is similar in that pre-tax money goes into an RRSP. Tax is deferred, but ultimately tax must be paid once the money leaves the RRSP. To learn more about the specific details of RRSPs, please visit: *http://www.cra-arc.gc.ca/tx/ndvdls/tpcs/rrsp-reer/rrsps-eng.html*.

TAX ADVANTAGED

Tax advantaged means you generally won't pay tax when you withdraw money from your account. Tax-advantaged investment money is after-tax money because you have already paid taxes on it.

Roth IRAs, 529 College Savings plans, TFSAs, and Life Insurance are popular investment vehicles that get tax-exempt distributions.

In Canada, Tax Free Savings Accounts (TFSAs) enjoy tax exemption (contributions are made with post-tax dollars, but no tax is paid when withdrawals are made). RESPs and RDSPs have some features that are "Tax Later" and "Tax Exempt". For more on the specific features of these plans, see: *http://www.cra-arc.gc.ca/tx/ndvdls/tpcs/tfsa-celi/menu-eng.html.*

BEFORE OR AFTER?

Should you avoid paying tax now and defer it until later when you get old?

Or should you pay now and not worry about tax in the future?

In other words, should you pay tax on the seed or pay tax on the harvest?

Let's take an example of Ms. A and Ms. B who both have $10,000 to invest at a 8% rate of return over 36 years. According to the Rule of 72, their money will double every 9 years.

Ms. A chooses to pay tax later, while Ms. B chooses a tax-advantaged vehicle and to pay tax now. Assume the current tax rate of both women is equal at 25%. Ms. A will start with $10,000 pre-tax money, and Ms. B will start with $7,500 after-tax money. Both are 29 years old.

Age	Tax Later Ms. A	Tax Advantaged Ms. B
29	$10,000	$7,500
38	$20,000	$15,000
47	$40,000	$30,000
56	$80,000	$60,000
65	$160,000	$120,000

At 65, Ms. A now has to pay tax. At this time, however, the tax rate may have changed.

- ✦ If the tax rate is the same at 25%:

    $160,000 - $40,000 (25% of $160,000) = **$120,000**

    Ms. A and Ms. B are equal.

- ✦ If the tax rate lowers to 15%:

    $160,000 - $24,000 (15% of $160,000) = **$136,000**

    Ms. A is ahead of Ms. B.

- ✦ If the tax rate hikes up to 35%:

    $160,000 - $56,000 (35% of $160,000) = **$104,000**

    Ms. A loses to Ms. B.

Ms. B pays tax on the seed (25%). Ms. A pays later on the harvest (the taxes of which could be lower or higher than 25%).

Both Ms. A and Ms. B take a calculated risk, based on their prediction of their future tax rate when they finally withdraw their money.

Some people think like Ms. A. When they're old, they will make less money. So they will pay a lower tax rate.

However, others think like Ms. B. With the trends of an aging population and higher budget deficits, the government will raise taxes.

People like Ms. B also believe they may still make good income in the future. They would rather pay taxes now on the seed and not worry about taxes when they harvest the big crop later.

Not all strategies work the same for everybody. It takes financial understanding and proper planning to find a good solution for your personal financial goals.

CAN YOU BUILD WEALTH?

Retirement was not always an urgent issue. Most of us don't often think about it, not to mention plan for it. In the past, life expectancy was short. Older generations died young or didn't live too long after retirement. So why would they worry?

U.S. Life Expectancy 1850-2011
White Male, newborn

1850	38
1900	48
1930	59
1960	67
1990	72
2011	76

During the 1800s, the average American had a short lifespan, topping out at 38. Lifespans extended after World War II and rose to 76 in 2011.* Future generations are expected to live into their 90s, maybe even longer. Chances are they will need a lot of money, or they will face a long life of financial distress.

Retirement saving and wealth building are a numbers game.

MONEY + TIME (+/-) RATE OF RETURN – INFLATION – TAX = WEALTH

As you look at the wealth formula, it shows you a guide to building wealth.

1. Spend less. Save more.

2. Invest your money long enough to allow interest to compound and for wealth to potentially build up.

3. The rate of return is very important.

4. Your money must earn a rate of return higher than inflation.

5. Look for investment vehicles that have tax advantages.

6. The result is your wealth: your future retirement.

Many people understand these concepts and work on it. You can do it too.

http://www.infoplease.com/ipa/A0005140.html

DEBT MANAGEMENT

Control your debt, or debt will control you.

Consider this. Say you have a credit card balance of $5,000 with 18% interest. If you pay $200 per month (minimum 4%), it will take 32 months, or almost 3 years, to pay it off.* And that assumes you don't add more debt to it.

So how many credit cards do you have? What about mortgages, student loans, car loans, and personal loans? Once you get yourself in debt, it will be hard to get out. Some people never escape.

Debt can turn into a disease. It could control your life, diminish your happiness, and limit your freedom.

Getting out of debt may be one of the hardest things to do and takes a lot of effort and time. But you must fight to do it. You can never be free until you are debt free.

Don't Get More Debt

Live below your means. You can't spend more than you make.

Don't Carry Credit Cards

Use cash, debit, or prepaid credit cards. When not using credit, you'll cut down your spending a lot. In some situations where you have to use a credit card, such as buying an airline ticket, make sure to pay off that purchase right away when you get the bill. You should cut up all your credit cards except one or two for convenience purposes.

Spend Money on Necessities

Pay only for what is necessary like food, the mortgage, insurance, and utilities. Cut out unnecessary expenses like cable TV and tech upgrades. You don't need hundreds of channels, expensive gadgets, or excess cell phone data.

There is no easy way. You have to give up something to get something.

Make a List of All Your Debt

Start to pay them off one at a time. Pick the easy, low-balance debt first and eliminate it. Like trimming bushes, cut them down one by one.

+ **Clear Smaller Debt First**
Once smaller debt is cleared, you have extra money to increase the dollar amount on monthly payments for your bigger debts. Using the previous example, if you pay $300 instead of $200 per month, you can pay off your credit card balance in 20 months instead of 32 months.

+ **Mortgage Prepayment**
If you have a 30-year mortgage at 4.5% interest for $300,000, your monthly payment is $1,520.06. If you put an additional $500 into these payments, you can pay off your mortgage in 18 years and 2 months.** How incredible is that! You would eliminate almost 12 years of debt. So when you get a raise, instead of celebrating your success with a nicer car, use the extra cash to prepay your mortgage. You'll get out of debt sooner and live a worry-free life.

*https://www.creditkarma.com/calculators/debtrepayment
**http://www.bankrate.com/calculators/mortgages/mortgage-calculator.aspx

THE X-CURVE CONCEPT
Building Wealth With Responsibility

The X-Curve concept is a simple way to show the relationship between taking care of your responsibility and building your wealth.

This concept theorizes that in general a person's responsibility decreases and their wealth increases over time.

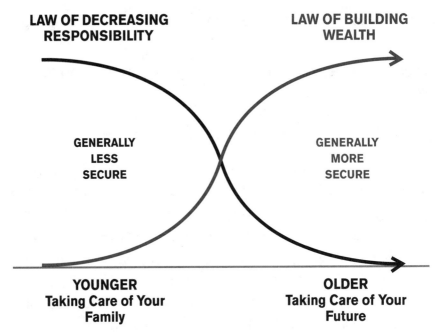

The X-Curve involves two curves that run at opposite directions during your lifetime.

THE WEALTH CURVE

When you're younger, you normally don't have money. Then you start to save and invest. As you build up your wealth, the wealth curve rises. Hopefully, when you get older, you have enough money for your retirement. The wealth curve is your investment curve.

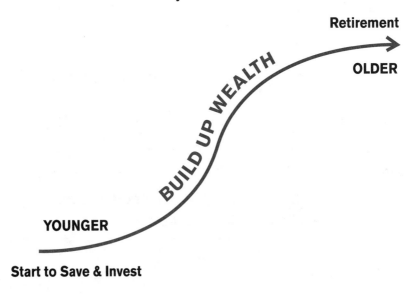

THE RESPONSIBILITY CURVE

However, when you are younger and start a new family, you have high responsibilities for:

✦ Children,

✦ Mortgage,

✦ College/university saving,

✦ Debts.

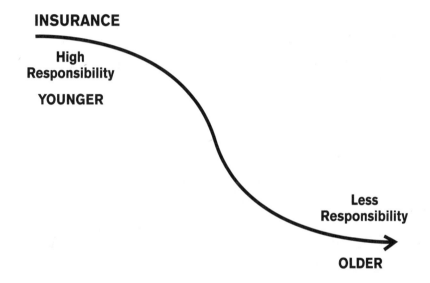

You and your spouse are responsible for these obligations whether you live or die. Early on, the need for insurance protection is quite high. But as your children grow up, your mortgage matures, and you reduce your debt, your responsibility will decrease.

MORE WEALTH, LESS RESPONSIBILITY

Assume you have 2 kids. If something happens to you, your spouse may not be able to take care of them alone. Factoring in your standard of living, your debts and savings goals, you figure out that you need $500,000 of protection. With $500,000 life insurance coverage, your spouse will be able to have enough income to raise the children in case you are gone.

However, let's say you are a good saver. You build up your wealth rapidly. When you have $100,000 saved, you may not need $500,000 of insurance. At that point, you only need $400,000 because if something happens, your spouse will have $100,000 savings plus $400,000 of insurance, totaling $500,000.

When you save $300,000, your protection need drops to $200,000. And of course, when you reach $500,000 of savings or investments on hand, you will no longer have the need for protection.

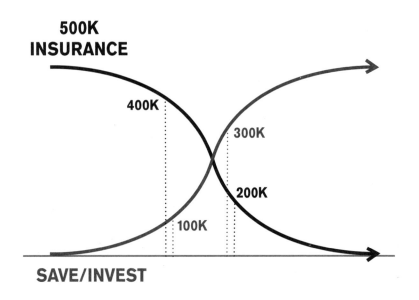

Let's apply this principle to your home. When you buy a house, your friend will come to the housewarming party and congratulate you, the new homeowner. But actually you don't own the home; the bank lender does. You own the mortgage, which is your responsibility. Until you pay it off, you don't own the home.

Assume your mortgage is $300,000 for 30 years. Most of your payments in the early years will go to interest payments and a little into the principal of the loan.

Understanding the X-Curve concept, you decide to pay more than the monthly payment in order to accelerate contributions to the principal of the loan. The faster you do that, the sooner you will be able to reduce your mortgage balance, and you can own your home sooner than scheduled.

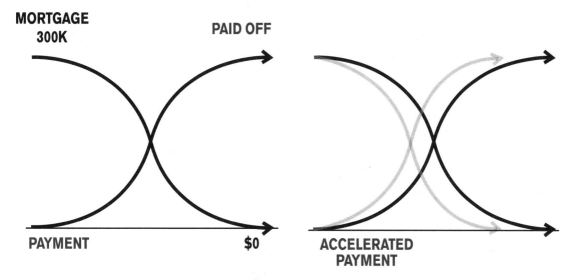

The X-Curve provides a clear approach for building your financial foundation. You'll be motivated to save, invest, and accumulate your assets faster, so you can reduce your debt, mortgage, and liability sooner. You will focus more on college funding and retirement, fulfilling your responsibility and reducing your insurance need.

In life, 2 outcomes can happen to you: Either you live too long or you die too soon. In any event, you should protect yourself and your family's future.

1. Have high protection when you are younger. It will take care of your family–children, college education, mortgage, debts–if something happens to you.

2. Save as much as you can to take care of your future.

Caution: There are a growing number of people who have more debt as they get older. Instead of reducing their mortgage, many people buy bigger houses and take on bigger mortgages. And of course, some may have more children if they remarry. As a result, they still have high responsibility and therefore high protection needs.

By understanding the X-Curve concept, you may want to decrease your responsibility and increase your saving to move toward a debt-free, happier life.

X-CURVE FOR THE RESPONSIBLE

The true meaning behind the X-Curve is responsibility. If people are not responsible, this concept is of no benefit.

There are people who spend hundreds of dollars a month drinking, partying, and gambling but have no insurance. Others shop until they drop on plastic money. Parents spoil their kids with toys and lavish birthdays, yet they save nothing into their college funding. Their popularity and their image to their friends take a higher priority than the future of their family.

The person with responsibility knows where his or her priority is: their family's financial future.

You must know what you want and what you need. You have a clear goal and a plan to achieve it.

Quite often, the person who doesn't care about protection for the family also doesn't worry much about saving for a rainy day. If they die too soon, their family will suffer. And if they live too long, many become a burden to their children.

But for the people who care for their family, if they die too soon, they'll have enough insurance protection for their loved ones. They also believe in saving for their children's college education. And if they live too long, they have enough savings to take care of themselves in their later years.

Without responsibility, there is no insurance need and no saving. There is no X-Curve.

INSURANCE OR INVESTMENT?

Insurance is for protection if something happens to you. Investment is for planning your family's future.

Insurance and investment may seem different, but they can be very similar, depending on how you look at it.

When you buy a house, you want to insure it. For example, you pay $500 per year to insure a $500,000 house. Even if you just pay a few years, if the house burns down, you'll get $500,000 to rebuild. You can say that $500 insurance is a good investment to cover your house.

If you are very young and have lots of responsibility, you want to pay $500 per year premium for life insurance that will protect your family with $500,000 death benefit. You can look at it as an expense, or you can look at it as an investment.

On the flip side, when you invest, the day you have $1,000,000 in your account, you won't need any life insurance. You can say that you are now self-insured.

Thus, insurance and investment are like two sides of a coin. When you are young, you need a lot of insurance. You want to invest some money to get big protection for your family. And when you are older and you have big investment, you're self-insured.

Whether you put your money into either insurance or investment, it can travel 2 different paths. But in the end the goal is to arrive at the same destination, your financial independence.

UNDERSTAND LIFE INSURANCE

Today, people have all kinds of protection. They insure their house, cars, phones, and appliances. They even buy travel insurance for their vacations.

But when it comes to life insurance, people remain skeptical. The most important insurance that protects their family and their children is not taken seriously.

Life insurance isn't a fun topic, but it's a critical part of your financial strategy. People don't often talk about it. Most don't understand it. Few want to buy it. Even those people who buy it don't necessarily understand it or appreciate its importance in building and preserving wealth. As a result, a lot of people don't have any life insurance protection. If they do, most don't have enough.

Life insurance doesn't insure your life. It insures your family's ability to continue on without being financially devastated.

A good number of people believe that they won't die anytime soon. Why would they need life insurance?

Some take it easy by just signing up with their employer's group life insurance. There's no need for a medical check up. Others get it free from their company. However, the company may not provide enough coverage, and if their employment terminates, they won't have protection. They may also have difficulties buying individual life insurance if they have medical problems and need more coverage.

ARE YOU INSURABLE?

Most life insurance requires medical exams, blood tests, and/or health records before a policy is issued. If you have health problems, life insurance companies may deny your application, or they may charge a higher rate. This is similar to how car insurance treats drivers with bad driving records.

A lot of people are not insurable and may not know it. An estimated 80 million Americans have 1 or more types of heart disease.[*] 1 out of 2 men and 1 out of 3 women have the risk of developing cancer in their lifetime.[**] Canadians face similar health issues, with 90% of Canadians having at least 1 risk factor for heart disease or stroke.[***]

Thus, if you have the need, buy life insurance as soon as you can while you're healthy and insurable. Buying early is also wise because you may qualify for better rates.

Don't wait too long, because when you have a health issue it may be too late. You might find out that you are no longer insurable.

Some policies can be issued without a medical exam or with limited medical questions. These forms of "guaranteed" policies typically charge higher premiums and are only available on lower coverage amounts.

[*]http://millionhearts.hhs.gov/abouthds/cost-consequences.html
[**]http://www.cancer.org/cancer/cancerbasics/lifetime-probability-of-developing-or-dying-from-cancer
[***]http://www.heartandstroke.com/site/c.iklQLcMWJtE/b.3483991/k.34A8/Statistics.htm

HOW MUCH LIFE INSURANCE?

Buying car insurance is simple. If your car is worth $35,000, you need $35,000 of coverage to cover the car in the event of a total loss.

Same with your house, if the value of the house is $300,000, you'll need $300,000 of coverage in case of disaster.

Most people can't apply the same valuation with life insurance simply because they don't know how to calculate how much they need.

THE DIME METHOD

Many people buy policies worth $100,000, $200,000, or $300,000, but that may not be enough. The DIME method offers an easy formula to calculate your life insurance protection need: DIME stands for debt, income, mortgage, and education.

How to Calculate Your Protection Need

Example of a hypothetical case
Client 1

Debt	**$50,000**	*[Combined credit cards, loans, and other debts.]*
Income	**$360,000**	*[$3K/mo. ($36K/yr.) income replacement for 10 years.]*
Mortgage	**$200,000**	*[Mortgage balances.]*
Education	**$120,000**	*[Assuming $15K/yr. for a 4-year college for 2 kids.]*
TOTAL	**$730,000**	***Protection Needed***

Most people have good protection on their house and cars, but few have enough for their loved ones.

With $730,000 of insurance protection, if this person dies too soon, the surviving spouse will have enough money to pay off $50,000 of debt, continue to have $3,000 income per month for 10 years or more, pay off the remaining $200,000 of their mortgage, keep the house, and still have $120,000 saved up for the 2 kids when they are ready for college.

The good news is with the DIME method you will know how to calculate your insurance need. The bad news is many will realize they don't have enough protection for their family.

According to the Life Insurance and Market Research Association (LIMRA), only 44% of U.S. households have individual life insurance, and the coverage is often not enough.** People say, "I already have life insurance!" They may, but the real question is do they have enough?

How would you feel if your $300,000 house burns to the ground and when you file a claim, your insurer tells you that you only have $50,000 worth of coverage? That normally wouldn't happen because your bank always makes sure you have $300,000 of protection.

What about your life and if you pass away? How would your spouse and kids feel when they receive a check for $100,000? After expenses, they may be left with very little and face a bleak future.

*The DIME Method is only one method to help determine a client's insurable need. However, an insurable need of more than 10 times the clients' current income may not be accepted by TFG unless special exceptions apply.
**http://www.limra.com/uploadedFiles/limracom/Posts/PR/LIAM/PDF/Facts-Life-2013.pdf
***Individual situations may vary. Individuals should always consult with their insurance agent/professional to ensure that they have proper protection that meets their unique needs.

DO STAY-AT-HOME PARENTS NEED LIFE INSURANCE?

Yes, they do. They may need a lot more than they think.

A lot of people think life insurance is for the breadwinner only. But stay-at-home parents should have protection to replace their valuable services to their family. Without them, these services can cost a lot. They are the driver, the cook, the cleaner, the teacher, and the accountant for the family. Without them, it could cost a lot of money to hire people to do their job. In most cases, the monetary value of their services is as high as if they had a full-time job. According to Salary.com, a "stay-at-home" parent is worth $112,962 per year.*

*http://www.salary.com/stay-at-home-mom-infographic

DO SINGLE PEOPLE NEED LIFE INSURANCE?

Most people buy life insurance to take care of their spouse and children. However, single people buy life insurance for different reasons.

✦ They have loved ones to take care of, such as their parents or less fortunate siblings.

✦ They may have a friend or relative who co-signed a student loan or mortgage. The co-signers will be on the hook if they're gone.

✦ They may start a family soon and want to buy when the cost is lower or while they are still healthy and insurable.

✦ They are in a business partnership and want to protect the business.

✦ They want to take advantage of the tax benefits of saving in the policy and have coverage at the same time.

✦ They want to leave a legacy to the cause they're passionate about.

HOW TO BUY LIFE INSURANCE

Many people find that buying life insurance is confusing. But actually it's not so complicated to understand.

Buying life insurance is no different than the many other things you buy daily. You buy it by its unit cost.

For example:

	COST	UNIT
Sugar	60 cents/$1.32	pound/kilogram
Eggs	$2	dozen
Gas	$3/80 cents	gallon/litre
Gold	$1,100/$39	ounce/gram
Movie	$12	ticket
Life Insurance	COI	$1,000 Insurance

COST PER $1,000

The cost of insurance (COI) per $1,000 coverage (or death benefit) for 1 year is the unit cost.*

For example: The COI per $1,000 for a 35-year-old male non-smoker is $1. This means that this man can pay $1 to get $1,000 insurance coverage for 1 year, or $1 per unit.

So if he buys a $100,000 insurance policy, he would buy 100 units, which is $1 x 100 = $100 for one year. If he needs $250,000, then he needs to buy 250 units. Thus, $1 x 250 = $250 for one year.

However, next year the COI per $1,000 will go up. As he gets older, the risk increases, and so does the price.

Age	COI/1,000	100k Policy		
35	$1	$1 x 100	=	$100/year
36	$1.10	$1.10 x 100	=	$110/year
37	$1.20	$1.20 x 100	=	$120/year
38	$1.35	$1.35 x 100	=	$135/year
39	$1.50	$1.50 x 100	=	$150/year

As he ages into his later years, the cost escalates greatly.

Age	COI/1,000	100k Policy
45	$3	$300
60	$8	$800
75	$25	$2,500

*Cost of Insurance – Charge varies based on the Insured's Age, Underwriting Classification and gender, and the Policy's Face Amount and duration. The company has the right to change current charges and cost of insurance rates. Any changes to charges or rates will be based on expectations to future cost facts. Such cost factors may include, but are not limited to, mortality, interest, persistency, expenses, reinsurance costs and state and federal taxes.
**All guarantees associated with a policy are based on the claims paying ability of the issuing company.

TERM INSURANCE

The following discussion while being general in nature provides a good foundation in understanding how insurance works. The concepts apply equally in the U.S. and Canada.

Insurance policies are based on the cost of insurance (COI).

The cost goes up every year because your risk of dying is higher as you get older.

It is also based on your health. For example, whether you smoke or not affects your rate. And if you're female, your rate is lower due to having better life expectancy.

Some refer to it as temporary insurance because it has a term or set period of coverage. And you have different kinds of terms. Generally, there are 3 kinds of Term Insurance.

Annual Renewable Term (ART)

Coverage is for a one-year term, renewable every year with a higher price. It costs much less when you're young but will be very expensive when you are old.

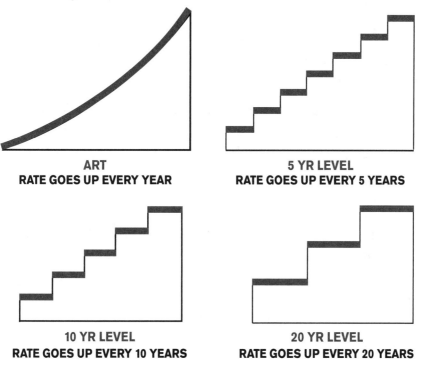

ART
RATE GOES UP EVERY YEAR

5 YR LEVEL
RATE GOES UP EVERY 5 YEARS

10 YR LEVEL
RATE GOES UP EVERY 10 YEARS

20 YR LEVEL
RATE GOES UP EVERY 20 YEARS

Level Term: 5, 10, 20, 30 years

The amount paid for coverage is the same or "level" for the term (for example, 5 years). However, at the end of each term, the cost increases, typically much more than ART. The insurance company averages the cost of insurance for the term. For example, in the above case, the COI goes from $1 at age 35 to $1.50 at age 39. So they may charge $1.25 for 5 years.

Decreasing Term

Normally sold as Mortgage Life Insurance, the premium cost will not increase during the entire life of the mortgage. The death benefit will pay off the balance of the mortgage. Thus, if something happens to you, the house will be paid off for the surviving spouse. Sounds good, right?

Mortgage Life Insurance is still Term Life. However, since the balance of the loan will decrease every year, the benefit decreases accordingly. Thus, you're buying a decreasing term.

Make sure you look at the cost. Quite often, you can get better rates with Level Term, and the benefit will remain constant—and not decrease—during that term.

Return of Premium Term

The policy will return the premium paid for the coverage if the insured survives the policy's term.

For example, say you pay $1,000 per year for $500,000 coverage in a 20-year Return of Premium Term policy. After 20 years, if nothing happens to your life, you will get back the $20,000 that you paid.

This type of term may cost you more and may have taxable implications, so make sure you know the costs to make a good decision.

Term Insurance is simple insurance. You pay the insurance company. If you die, they pay the benefit to your family. If you don't die, they don't pay, and you lose the premium money, just like car insurance.

Is Your Term Renewable?

Be aware that some term policies are not renewable.

Many term polices are renewable. It means you are guaranteed to renew the term for the rest of your life regardless of your health condition. But with Non-Renewable Term, you may not be able to renew unless you have good health. Of course, Non-Renewable is usually cheaper than renewable term.

Is Your Term Convertible?

Convertible insurance policies allow the insured to convert to another policy, usually from term to permanent life, regardless of the insured's health.

Most often, this conversion privilege applies to employees who have Group Term Life when they end their employment. The conversion period is typically 31 days after termination. However, many people fail to follow through.

PERMANENT LIFE: TERM + CASH

Also called cash value life insurance, there are different types of permanent life.

Whole Life

It's the original and oldest form of cash value life insurance. Instead of paying just the cost of insurance, you pay higher premiums. The difference between the cost of insurance and the premium goes into your cash value. Whole Life policies give you a guaranteed rate of interest. Some insurance companies may provide dividends, but dividends are not guaranteed.

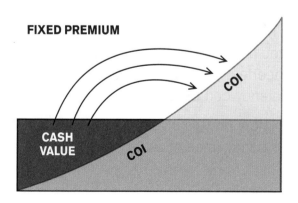

The cash value compounded with interest built up in the early years will pay for the higher COI in the later years, so the policy can last a whole lifetime.

Whole Life is typically not very flexible. The premium is fixed, the interest guaranteed, and the death benefit fixed. Since insurance companies have to guarantee the interest for the whole life, they tend to give a conservative rate. As a result, the cash build up can be slow.

It should be noted that these types of policies may have surrender charges (fees associated with canceling the policy in the early years). These are long-term ("whole life") products.

BUY TERM, INVEST THE DIFFERENCE

Many people say, "Why bother with cash value life?", especially Whole Life, when you can use a strategy such as "Buy Term and invest the difference".

It questions why you should pay, for example, $1,000 a year for Whole Life when you can just pay $200 for Term Insurance for the same coverage? You can invest the difference ($800) into another investment (such as a mutual fund) to get a better potential rate of return. And you can use that investment to pay for the higher cost of insurance in the later years, or you can use it for retirement.

There are a lot of believers in this logic, and quite a few of them converted their Whole Life policies to buy Term.

However, in order for this theory to work, 2 conditions must be met.

1. You must have the discipline and consistency to invest the difference. If not, you may end up buying Term but spending the difference. With uncertainty about the economy and the ever-changing jobs market, consistency can be a challenge.

2. You must know how to invest the difference. Other investments may be able to give better rates of return, but they may also sink your nest egg.

In either case, if your investments haven't performed well at the end of the term, and the cost of insurance substantially increases, you may have lost your surplus money, or even worse, you may no longer be able to afford to continue your insurance coverage.

Thus, consider all options to find a suitable solution for your financial foundation.

ADDITIONAL LIFE INSURANCE PRODUCTS AVAILABLE IN THE U.S.

Universal Life

The difference between Universal Life and Whole Life is its flexibility. You can change your premium. You can pay more one month or less the next. Sometimes when you face money problems, you can even skip a few payments as long as the cash value inside the policy is enough to pay for the COI.

You can adjust your death benefit to fit with life-changing conditions. The interest on the cash value may also be sensitive to market conditions. That allows insurance companies to adjust the interest rate to give higher or lower rates if necessary. Some UL policies also provide a minimum guaranteed interest.

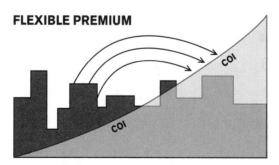

FLEXIBLE PREMIUM

Index Universal Life

Index Universal Life (IUL) is a fast-growing product due to its index strategy. Since it's a UL, it has all of its flexible features.

The key part of this product is the cash value is based on a certain index, such as the S&P 500. The investor is not directly investing into the index. Instead, the cash value inside the policy is credited with a return based on the performance of the index.

You can earn growth based on the index, but only up to a ceiling maximum, called a cap, for example, 13%. However, if the index drops, you have the safety that you won't go lower than a minimum floor, for example, 0%. So if the S&P 500 drops 20% negative, you get 0% interest. That's the minimum floor, which means your cash value doesn't lose any money during a down market. And if it gains 15%, you can only get 13% return at the maximum cap.

Other types of life insurance include Variable Life and Variable Universal Life. These investment-related products are discussed in later chapters.

THE INDEX UNIVERSAL LIFE STRATEGY

In an effort to cut down the impact of losses, some insurance products began to introduce a new strategy using market indexes such as the S&P 500. Let's take a look at the following examples.

Example 1: $100 per year is put into this account.

End of year	Return	Total
1	+12%	$112
2	-12%	$98.56
3	+12%	$110.39
4	-12%	$97.14

Example 2: Same amount, but no negative return.

End of year	Return	Total
1	12%	$112
2	0%	$112
3	12%	$125.44
4	0%	$125.44

With the same account, if you replace any negative return with 0%, which is $0 lost for those years, the end result will be much better.

Please note that the above examples are for conceptual explanation purposes. They do not include fees, costs, or charges. Thus, the actual result will be lower.

The S&P 500 Index is a broad measure of the U.S. stock market. Indices are unmanaged, and one cannot invest directly in an index.

ADDITIONAL LIFE INSURANCE PRODUCTS AVAILABLE IN CANADA

The insurance industry saw that there was a need for products that were more flexible and allowed for more sophistication to meet the needs of consumers. From this, **Universal Life (UL)** was born.

Universal Life, like Whole Life, is generally intended to provide protection for a lifetime and accumulate a cash value. Unlike Whole Life, ULs permit a variety of different investment options, many of which may have the potential to outperform the guarantees offered by a traditional Whole Life policy.

Additionally, ULs may be a useful tool in implementing some tax and/or estate strategies, may allow for changes to the death benefit, and may provide some flexibility in the timing of premium payments. ULs also tend to be more transparent, in that the different fees and COI are broken out.

Segregated Funds (or individual variable insurance contracts) are another insurance option available to Canadians. These products combine life insurance coverage with investments such as mutual funds. These products also typically have an investment guarantee that promises that the client will receive a minimum portion of their initial investment (for example, 75%).

Segregated funds may also provide protection from creditors. These products are best reviewed with your insurance agent who can help you navigate all of the different features and options available.

WHICH ONE SHOULD YOU CHOOSE?

Term, WL, UL, or IUL?

You probably have a similar dilemma when buying a car. Should you buy a sedan, a SUV, a minivan, or a pick up truck?

To the mechanic, all cars are similar. They share the same basics: an engine, a transmission, and 4 wheels plus a steering wheel. The difference is what they put on top of it, and you pick the one that fits your needs.

If they add a flatbed, they call it a pick up truck.

If they have just 2 seats, a sports car.

If they have 4 doors, a sedan.

If they put 4 big wheels, a SUV.

And if they put in 3 rows of seating, a minivan.

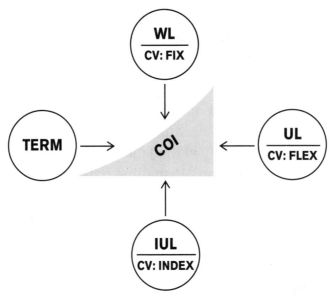

Likewise, the basics of all insurance is COI. But the cash value on top of it determines the different types.

If you pay the basic COI, it's Term.

If the cash value (CV) is fixed guarantee, it's Whole Life.

If the CV interest is market sensitive and flexible, it's UL.

If the CV is tied to the Index, it's IUL.

No matter what you call it, all insurance has one thing in common. You have to pay for the COI inside their policy, which is the cost of term insurance.

We can sum it up as follows:

1. All insurance is term insurance (COI).

2. The cost of term insurance always goes up.

3. There is no free lunch. You have to pay for it.

In other words, all insurance is either term or term plus cash. The COI always goes up as you get older. You must pay for the term insurance directly, or you must have enough money in the cash value to pay for it.

But I Was Told I Only Need to Pay for 8 Years

It's possible. If you pay a substantial amount of premium in the first 8 years, the big cash build up may be able to pay for the higher COI for the life of the policy.

In many cases, though, you may not have enough. Say you make regular payments, but the cash build up inside is small. When you stop at the 8th year, you have 2 options.

1. You keep the same coverage, but the policy will extend for a shorter period of time, not the rest of your life. When the policy runs out of money, it lapses, and you are no longer insured.

2. You can use that small cash value as a single premium to buy a smaller policy, with a smaller coverage amount for the rest of your life.

Again, there is no free lunch. You pay more; you get more. You pay less; you get less.

IS IT SUITABLE? IS IT AFFORDABLE?

At the end of the day, when you have to make a decision, whatever you buy, you should buy what you need and what you can afford. In other words, is the product suitable and affordable for you?

First, you must find out what you need. Calculate your protection need (the coverage amount). Then assess your financial situation.

Rearrange your budget and cut down unnecessary expenses if you must. Then you can make a better decision.

If you have high responsibility but not much money, term may be a better choice for you. If you have enough money to cover your need and savings as well, you may want to look into other options with cash build up that fit with your savings and investment goals.

OTHER TYPES OF LIFE INSURANCE

Accidental Death Insurance

This insurance can be a stand-alone option but is often added to an existing life insurance policy. Also known as double indemnity coverage, it covers only accident-related deaths, unlike regular life insurance, which covers all causes of death.

For example, say you have a life insurance policy with a $100,000 death benefit plus an additional $100,000 Accidental Death rider. If you die from regular illness, they will pay $100,000 only. But if your death is caused by accident, they will pay $200,000.

If you need $500,000 of coverage, make sure to get that amount of coverage in an individual plan. Don't hope that you have to die by accident to get the right benefit.

Joint Life Insurance

Joint life insurance generally covers 2 people, typically a married couple. There are 2 types of joint policies typically available, First to die and Second (last) to die. A Second to die policy does not pay the benefit until the death of the last surviving spouse. A First to die policy pays out when the first person passes away.

A common purpose of this type of insurance is to protect a business. Most often it's for estate planning because the benefit is used to minimize or eliminate the burden of estate tax on the heirs. The cost of this type of policy is usually cheaper than if the couple had bought 2 separate policies.

Key Person Insurance

It's simply a life insurance policy on the key person in a business. Normally, it applies to the owner or key employee, people who are very important to the business. If something were to happen to them, the company or business may not survive.

The company buys the life insurance on these key persons, pays the premium, and is the beneficiary of the policy.

Executive Bonus Life Insurance

This is a life insurance policy offered to an executive in a company. The company pays the premium and can deduct it as a tax-exempt contribution. The executive receives the benefit.

With Executive Bonus policies that have cash value, the executive can take out loans against the policy. However, he or she must claim the premium payment as regular income. In the event the executive passes away, the family will receive the benefit.

Executive Bonus is a good way for employers to attract or keep their important employees.

Final Expense Insurance

Also referred to as Funeral expense insurance, this insurance is used to pay for funeral costs. This gives some peace of mind to those in their final days without creating an additional financial burden to their loved ones.

For people who may not qualify for regular life insurance, this product is handy due to simplified and easier underwriting. In many cases, people who have medical issues may still have a chance to qualify.

LIVING BENEFITS OF LIFE INSURANCE

The main purpose of life insurance is to protect your loved ones, business, or estate if you die. However, in many cases, the insured may have great needs at critical times while still living.

Living benefits, also known as Accelerated Death Benefits, are a feature where the insurance company pays or advances a portion of the policy's death benefit to the insured to pay for care or treatment. If the insured dies, the balance of the death benefit will then be paid to the beneficiary.

In cases of serious illness such as heart disease, stroke, cancer, paralysis and terminal illness with diagnosis for less than 12 months to live, the accelerated payments will be very helpful for the insured and family.

Thus, life insurance is beneficial not just for the death benefit. With living benefits, the insurance can be more flexible to provide much needed money at critical times.

Many Term Life policies have this benefit. It can also be purchased as a rider in permanent life policies.*

*Riders and rider benefits have specific limitations and costs and may not be available in all jurisdictions. Review any life insurance policy you are considering for complete details, including the terms and conditions of riders and exact coverage provided.

TAX ADVANTAGES OF LIFE INSURANCE

Under current Internal Revenue Service (IRS) and Canada Revenue Agency (CRA) guidelines, insurance policies receive many favorable tax advantages.

Tax-Free Death Benefit

Should the insured die, the entire death benefit including the cash value is income-tax free to the beneficiary.

Tax-Deferred Earnings

You do not pay taxes on gains in the policy. Tax is deferred until you decide to surrender the policy, the policy has lapsed, or when certain distributions occur.

Tax-Free Withdrawals

When the cash value in the policy is sufficient, premiums paid into a policy can be taken as tax-free withdrawals up to your cost basis in the policy. This is the premium you paid with after-tax dollars.

Tax-Free Loans

Besides the withdrawals, you can take more money out of the policy in excess of your basis (your paid premiums) through tax-free loans with a very low net effective rate.

When you take a loan from the insurance company, they will take the same amount of the loan from your cash value and transfer it to a loan reserve account. They will charge you interest on the loan (for example, 3%). However, the loan reserve earns interest (for example, 2%). In sum, they loan their money to you at 3%, but the same amount of your money in the reserve account earns 2%, so you actually pay a net rate of 1%. This is an excellent feature when you need to access your money.

As long as you stay within the IRS guidelines, the withdrawals and loans can be taken without federal income tax liability.*

In Canada, insurance policies generally receive favorable tax treatment, and funds are sheltered from taxes. Individuals should consult with their tax professional and their insurance agent for additional information, specifically in regards to policy loans.

*Loans and withdrawals can only be made if the policy has been in force long enough and has accumulated sufficient value. Loans and withdrawals will reduce the cash value and death benefit and loans are subject to interest charges. Policy loans are generally not taxable when taken. If a policy is surrendered or lapses while a loan is outstanding, adverse consequences may result. Cash withdrawals are also not generally taxable until they exceed the basis in the policy. However, if the policy is treated as a modified endowment contract (MEC) by IRS Sec. 7702A, withdrawals and loans are taxable at an ordinary income tax rate when taken to the extent of gain in the contract and may be subject to a 10% federal income tax penalty if taken prior to age 59½. Cash distributions associated with benefit reduction, including reductions caused by withdrawals during the first 15 years, may be taxable. Consult with your tax professional regarding your situation.

THE IMPORTANCE OF TAX ADVANTAGES

The tax advantages of insurance are only good if you have gains and a significant accumulation of money.*

If you have Term, all these tax-free loans, tax-free withdrawals, and tax-deferred earnings are of no use because term has no cash.

For those with Permanent Life, if you have little money in it, it also makes little difference.

In reality, many policy owners either don't understand the advantages, don't have the money, or don't want to contribute enough to capitalize on the tax advantages.

Also, in the past, traditional policies with low rates of interest did not help to accumulate high cash values, so these advantages were not so beneficial.

But with the recent introduction of different savings and investment choices, more people are able to get better cash accumulation and make good use of these tax advantages.

Considering the amount of taxes people pay, people must understand and look for the vehicles, whether in insurance or investment, that can save their future cash build up.

The authors of this book and companies referenced do not give tax or legal advice. This material and concepts presented here are for informational purposes and should not be construed as tax or legal advice. This material was not intended or written to be used, and cannot be used, to avoid penalties imposed under the Internal Revenue Code. This material was written in whole or in part to support the promotion or marketing of the transaction(s) or matter(s) addressed in this material. Anyone to whom any transaction or concept addressed in this material is promoted, marketed, or recommended should seek and rely on advice based on the person's particular circumstances from an independent tax advisor.

UNDERSTANDING ANNUITIES

As more people are concerned about living a long life in retirement, annuities are becoming a solution for long-term planning. An annuity is the savings version of a life insurance product. All annuities are classified as either Deferred or Immediate.

Deferred Annuity

Deferred annuities are tax-deferred accounts where the owner invests a lump sum (such as from a rollover 401k or IRA) or makes regular payments over the course of many years. This period of cash growth and build up is called the accumulation phase.

Immediate Annuity

Immediate annuities are different. The owner puts in a lump sum and starts receiving payments right away based on the term of the annuity contract.

TWO PHASES IN AN ANNUITY

Accumulation Phase

The accumulation phase only applies to deferred annuities. During this time, your contributions gradually build up.

Early withdrawal during the accumulation phase may face a surrender charge. However, most annuities allow the policy holder to make partial withdrawals within their contract without penalty.

In the U.S., if withdrawing before age 59½, you may get a 10% federal income tax penalty as with other tax-deferred accounts.

Payout Phase

The payout phase is traditionally referred to as annuitization. When the owner receives payouts, the annuitization period begins. There are many options for payouts.

- ✦ **Period Certain:** You choose the period. Let's say 20 years. You receive payments for 20 years. If you die early after 12 years, the payout will continue the next 8 years to your beneficiary. If you still live past 20 years, it will stop at the 20th year.

- ✦ **Lifetime Payment:** You receive payments as long as you live. Payments stop when you die.

- ✦ **Lifetime Payment with Period Certain**–the combination of the above. Let's say you choose 25 years. If you die in the 20th year, the payment will continue for another 5 years to the beneficiary. If you live past the 25 years, the payments will continue until your death.

- ✦ **Joint and Survivor Annuities** are usually for couples. If one dies, the payment continues to the spouse until his or her last day.

In recent years, new annuity contracts have offered a rider called guaranteed lifetime income withdrawal. It does not require annuitization of contracts, which gives the client more flexibility at the payout phase.

It is important to understand that annuities can be an excellent tool if you use them properly. Annuities are not right for everyone.

ANNUITY: A REVERSE BET!

In a way, annuities look like a reverse life insurance policy.

The primary difference between an annuity and life insurance is when payment is made. Annuities pay a set amount of money monthly, quarterly, or annually to meet future financial needs, usually in retirement. Life insurance pays the value of the policy at the time of death.

With life insurance, you make a bet with the life insurance company. You make payments to the policy, for example, $1,000 per year, and if you die too soon, the company will pay the death benefit to your beneficiary. In this case, your family wins; the company loses.

With an annuity, you give them a lump sum or accumulated premium, for example, $500,000, and bet that you'll live a long time. If you live long enough, the company keeps paying you monthly. In that case, the company may end up paying you more than what you put into the annuity; thus, you win. But if you die too soon, the company wins because they will stop payment or only pay up to a certain period.

Thus, annuities are a good solution for people who worry that they may live too long and run out of money. Annuities can help them feel confident about their financial future.

Annuities offer different investment options.

✦ **Fixed Annuity:** Guarantees a fixed rate of return.*

✦ **Fixed Index Annuity:** Return is credited by a market index, such as the S&P 500. The index normally has a minimum floor and a maximum cap, for example 0% to 8%. Thus, if the S&P 500 goes higher than 8%, it will credit max 8%. And if the index has a loss, it will hit a 0% floor; there is no loss in the account.**

In the U.S., unlike IRAs and 401ks, annuities have no limits on contribution. You can put in as much as you want.

Also, due to lifetime payouts, it is a vehicle of choice for many people to rollover or transfer their 401k and IRA into annuities, so they can get the advantage of the payout phase.

The guarantees of fixed annuity contracts are contingent on the claims-paying ability of the issuing insurance company. Annuity withdrawals are taxed as ordinary income and may be subject to a 10% federal penalty if made prior to age 59½. Surrender charges may also apply during the policy's early years.

**Index Annuities are typically linked to a major stock market index, such as the Standard & Poor's Index of 500 common stocks, but do not represent direct participation in the stock market. Past performance of the S&P 500, or any other index that these types of annuities may be linked to, does not guarantee future results. In the event that any given index has a negative return, the issuer of the index annuity may credit a minimum interest rate guarantee, which is generally around 3%, or no interest may be credited. This will depend on the terms of the contract that can vary greatly from one contract to the next. You should also note that in some fixed index annuity contracts, the stated participation rate may not be credited at all if the annuity is not held to the contract term which may be several years.

***Generally, principal is guaranteed by the issuing insurer when the annuity is held to the end of the guarantee period. Guarantees are based on the claims paying ability of the issuing insurance company. Participation rates, caps or other components of the formula used to calculate credited rates vary and can change. Withdrawals prior to the end of the guarantee period may be subject to market value adjustments; therefore you may receive less than you originally invested. Withdrawals during the first several years are subject to surrender charges and withdrawals prior to age 59½ may be subject to a 10% federal tax penalty.

****Fixed index annuities can be complicated. Before you purchase an equity index annuity, read the contract and any sales literature and be sure that you completely understand all of the terms and provisions of any fixed index annuity you are considering.

THE CAPITAL MARKETS:
Stocks and Bonds

To know how money works, we should understand how the financial markets work. Generally, when a company needs to raise money, they can either issue stock or bond certificates.

The First Market

The company sells stock and bonds through a process called Initial Public Offering (IPO). During IPO, this is the first time these certificates are being offered to the public.

Stock and bond certificates are called securities.

The Secondary Market

After IPO, investors can buy, sell, and trade these certificates on the stock market. Among the world's stock markets, the New York Stock Exchange is the biggest.

STOCK

A stock is an instrument that signifies equity ownership in a corporation, and represents a proportionate claim on a company's assets and profits.

BONDS

A bond is an instrument of indebtedness of the bond issuer to the holders.

THE MARKET INDEX

Every time you turn on the TV or log onto the Internet, you'll often see the Dow Jones or the S&P 500.

These are stock market indexes. An index is a statistical indicator used to measure and report change in the market value of a group of stocks. The rising and falling of those numbers on any given day provide you an idea of how the index is performing and what the market is doing in general. Keep in mind, however, that market indexes are unmanaged, and it is not possible to invest directly in an index.

THE DOW

The Dow Jones Industrial Average (DJIA) is the most well-known index in the world. The Dow measures 30 powerful companies in America. Most people consider it the barometer of the U.S. stock market. However, it does not reflect smaller-sized companies.

DOW COMPONENTS AS OF JANUARY 2015

3M	Exxon Mobil	Microsoft
American Express	General Electric	Nike
AT&T	Goldman Sachs	Pfizer
Boeing	Home Depot	Proctor and Gamble
Caterpillar	IBM	Travelers
Chevron	Intel	United Technologies
Cisco Systems	Johnson and Johnson	UnitedHealth Group
Coca Cola	JP Morgan Chase	Verizon
Walt Disney	McDonald's	Visa
DuPont	Merck	Wal-Mart

S&P 500

The Standard & Poor's 500 is the indicator of 500 large cap companies and covers about 70% of the entire U.S. equity value. These companies represent all major sectors of the U.S. economy from manufacturing to financials, health care, tech, energy, retail, and pharmaceuticals. Thus, it better reflects the U.S. market than the Dow and is more frequently quoted by financial experts.

NASDAQ

The Nasdaq Composite Index lists the stocks of over 4,000 companies in its market. It's heavily weighted toward technology stocks with well-known names like Apple, Google, Microsoft, Cisco, Intel, Tesla, Netflix, and Amazon.

Outside the US, indexes track the stocks of big companies throughout the world, such as the Hang Seng in Hong Kong, Euro Stoxx 50 in Europe, and the Nikkei 225 in Japan.

The world is getting smaller. These indexes are highly observed and have global impact, affecting not only companies but economies all over the world.

MONEY MARKET

It's a market for short-term, low-risk securities such as U.S. Treasury Bills, bank CDs, commercial paper, and other debt issues by corporations or governments.

Money market accounts (MMA) are offered through banks or credit unions. It generally gives better returns than savings accounts and provides easy access to money when you need it. But it tends to require a higher deposit amount to participate.

MMAs are different than money market funds, which are mutual funds with money market portfolios.

MUTUAL FUNDS

When you invest for the long term, you must find investment vehicles that have the potential to grow to outpace inflation and achieve your purpose. Historically, the stock market over the long run performs better than conservative vehicles like T-Bills, bank CDs, GICs, or government bonds.

PERFORMANCE OF STOCKS, BONDS, AND T-BILLS FROM 1926 TO 2013
Compound annual return

Small cap stocks	**12.3%**
Large cap stocks	**10.1%**
Government bonds	**5.5%**
Treasury bills	**3.5%**

Source: Ibbotson SBBR
Past performance does not guarantee future results.

However, investing in securities like stocks and bonds can be a challenging task for most people.

Enter the mutual fund (MF). Begun in the late 1920s with just a handful of funds, mutual funds had a slow climb. By the 1960s, mutual funds gained traction, accelerating into huge numbers in the 80s. Today there are now over 7,000 funds in the U.S. and 5,000 in Canada.[*][**]

Mutual funds have become a popular way for the general public to participate in the stock market. Since August of 2000, assets under management in mutual funds even surpassed commercial banks.[***] Many pensions, 401ks, and IRAs invest in mutual funds. Thus, there is a good chance that you are already invested in a mutual fund.

However, few people have a solid understanding about mutual funds and how to use them to make better choices for their goals.

[*]*http://money.usnews.com/money/personal-finance/mutual-funds/articles/2013/06/10/are-there-too-many-mutual-funds*
[**]*http://www.desjardins.com/ca/co-opme/action-plans-tips/savings-investment/what-need-know-mutual-funds*
[***]*http://www.federalreserve.gov/pubs/bulletin/2000/1200lead.pdf*

HOW MUTUAL FUNDS WORK

Let's say you have $100 and want to invest. This small amount of money may only allow you to buy 1 share of 1 company stock, and the risk and reward of 1 stock is high.

If you have $1,000 and put $100 in 10 different stocks, you are starting to spread your risk out. Now consider if you have 1,000 people like you who also invest $1,000, then together you have $1,000,000. This large sum would greatly expand your investment choices.

A mutual fund is a pool of money from investors. Each fund has a specific mandate or purpose and a professional fund manager who invests the money based on the specific strategy and goal of the fund.

TYPES OF MUTUAL FUNDS

When it comes to mutual funds, investors have thousands of choices. The important thing is that you must know the risk and the investment purpose of each fund to make a proper decision. In general, mutual funds fall into 1 of the 4 major categories.

1. **Money Market Funds** are considered relatively low risk.

2. **Bond Funds** buy government and/or corporate bonds.

3. **Stock Funds** buy shares in companies.

4. **Balanced Funds** hold a mix of stocks and bonds.

Stock funds are quite popular, offering a wide range of funds, which can be identified by 4 main categories.

✦ **Growth Funds** focus more on capital appreciation.

✦ **Value Funds** focus more on stocks that are deemed to be undervalued in price and likely to pay regular dividends.

✦ **Index Funds** aim to achieve returns similar to a particular index such as the S&P 500.

✦ **Sector Funds** focus on a particular industry segment such as biotech, energy, real estate, emerging markets, etc.

In reality, mutual funds consist of a mix of stocks, bonds, money market and other assets, offering a wide variety of choices to investors.

BUYING AND SELLING MF SHARES
NAV: Net Asset Value

Net asset value (NAV) is similar to the stock price of a company. NAV measures the value of one share of the fund.

$$NAV = \frac{Assets - Liabilities}{Outstanding\ shares}$$

Example: Fund XYZ has 1,000,000 shares. At the end of trading day, it has $15,000,000 worth of securities, $2,000,000 in cash, and $1,000,000 in liabilities.

$$NAV = \frac{\$15M + \$2M - \$1M}{1M\ shares} = \$16$$

MUTUAL FUND FEES AND EXPENSES:
Load or No Load?

As with any business, running a mutual fund involves costs. Funds pass along these costs to investors by charging fees and expenses.

Fees and expenses vary from fund to fund. The fund with high costs must perform better than low-cost funds to generate the same return for you. Investors should always read the Fund Facts to see what the objectives of the fund are, its risk profile, and the fees and expenses it charges. The fund's simplified prospectus also contains information about risks, fees, and charges.

In the U.S., the Securities and Exchange Commission (SEC) requires funds to disclose these fees and charges as well as information about the mutual fund's objectives, risk, and performance in the prospectus.

Mutual fund charges include but are not limited to: front load, back end load, purchase fee, redemption fee, exchange fee, and account fee, plus annual operating expenses such as management fee, distribution/service fee ("12b-1 fees"), and other expenses.

A Word About "No-Load" Funds

Some funds call themselves "no-load". As the name implies, this means that the fund does not charge any type of sales load. But as discussed above, not every type of shareholder fee is a "sales load". A no-load fund may charge fees that are not sales loads, such as purchase fees, redemption fees, exchange fees, and account fees. No-load funds will also have operating expenses.*

Make sure you review the fee table of the fund you're considering, including no-load funds, to be aware of these charges.

*http://www.sec.gov/investor/pubs/inwsmf.htm

THE ADVANTAGES OF MUTUAL FUNDS

+ **Professional Management.** Money managers provide investment expertise in researching, selecting, and monitoring the performance of the securities purchases.

+ **Diversification.** Diversification lowers your risk by not putting all your eggs in one basket. The money will be spread among different stocks, bonds, and other assets.*

+ **Liquidity.** You can get in or out quite easily.

+ **Low investment minimums.** Some funds can let you start investing with as low as $50 a month.

+ **Ease and convenience.** It's easy to set up pre-authorized checking (PAC) programs for ongoing purchases and dollar cost averaging.

*Diversification cannot assure a profit or guarantee against loss in declining markets.

THE DISADVANTAGES

✦ The professionals can be wrong. There are no guarantees. You can lose money.

✦ Fees and expenses reduce your return.

HOW YOU CAN MAKE MONEY WITH MUTUAL FUNDS

There are 3 ways you can make money with mutual funds.

1. Income. Income returns to the fund from stock dividends and bond interest.

2. Capital gains distribution. The price of the securities a fund owns may increase when the fund sells them, in which case it has a capital gain. The gains will be distributed back to the investors.

3. Increased NAV. Investors can make money by selling mutual fund units at a price higher than they bought them.

Price (NAV) Appreciation

Income Distribution

Capital Gains Distribution

TOTAL INVESTMENT RETURN

Generally, any income or capital gain that an investor receives is taxed. Individuals should always consult with their tax professional and understand the effects that taxation may have on their investments.*.**

A mutual fund's yield, share price, and investment return will fluctuate so that investors may receive more or less than originally invested when shares are redeemed.

**Mutual funds are sold by prospectus. Before investing, consider any mutual fund's investment objectives, risks, charges and expenses. Contact your financial advisor for a prospectus containing this information. Read it carefully.

EXCHANGE TRADED FUNDS

An exchange-traded fund (ETF) is an investment fund traded on stock exchanges, much like stocks. ETFs hold assets such as stocks, commodities, or bonds, and fluctuates over the course of the trading day.

VARIABLE LIFE, VARIABLE UNIVERSAL LIFE, VARIABLE ANNUITY

Over the last several decades, the insurance industry has incorporated investment vehicles into their insurance products.

By combining investments with insurance, clients may be able to capitalize on the potential growth of the market while also benefitting from the tax advantages of life insurance and annuities.

These products offer many investment choices managed by professional managers in mutual fund-like portfolios. However, due to the nature of capital markets, the potential gain can be offset by potential loss. So the policy owner should understand their objective and their risk tolerance in purchasing these products.

Here are some products that have gained popularity in the past several decades.

Variable Life and Variable Universal Life

The difference between permanent life policies with cash, such as Whole Life and Variable Life (VL), is that the extra cash in the VL is put into a separate account, which is invested into securities, instead of the insurance policy's cash value.

The policy owner is responsible for the investment of this account. You can put this extra cash into different investment options. Therefore, if your underlying investments perform well, then your death benefit and cash value may increase accordingly. If your investments perform worse than you expected, your death benefit and cash value may decrease, and you may have to pay more into the policy to keep it in force.

Variable Universal Life (VUL) is very similar to Variable Life (VL), except that you have flexibility on the premium and the death benefit.*

In Canada, Universal Life policies offer both interest-bearing accounts as well as different investment options from various money management funds. Thus, up north, the Variable Life name is unnecessary.

Variable life insurance is a long-term product, which assesses certain fees and charges to include surrender charges during the first several years. Sub-account values will fluctuate with market conditions and may be worth more or less than their original cost upon redemption. Loans and withdrawals will reduce the cash value and death benefit, and loans are subject to interest charges. If a policy lapses while a loan is outstanding, adverse tax consequences may result.

Variable Annuity

When you put money into fixed annuities, the insurance company will give you a fixed rate of return.*

With variable annuities, the policy owner is responsible to choose different investment options for their money. Thus, your rate of return depends on the performance of your investments.

There are many investment choices, typically mutual fund-like portfolios. The account will gain or lose value depending on how it's invested in the market.

Since the main purpose of annuities for most people is to plan for their long-term retirement, it's extremely important that they are very careful in managing their portfolio and understanding the risks.

Generally, the older you are, the less risk you should take.**

The guarantees of fixed annuity contracts are contingent on the claims-paying ability of the issuing insurance company.
Variable annuity sub-account values will fluctuate with market conditions and when redeemed, may be worth more or less than the original cost.

Variable life and variable annuity products are sold by prospectus. Before investing, consider any variable product's investment objectives, risks, charges and expenses. Contact your financial advisor for a prospectus containing this information. Read it carefully.

CONSIDERATIONS WHEN INVESTING

Past performance is no indication of future results. This important phrase is displayed on every mutual fund prospectus.

When investing, keep in mind that all the data, statistics, rates of return, dividend yields, and share prices were numbers of the past.

Tomorrow is a different day. No one can predict future performance. No one knows where the market will go because no one will know how technology will change, whether war or natural disasters will strike, if there will be food surpluses or gas shortages, and so on.

So when you invest, this data is relatively helpful to give you an idea of how a certain investment vehicle has performed in the past. It is important for you to know your risk tolerance.

It's up to you to consider it and make a decision to apply it for your financial future.

TIME AND TIMING

Knowing Your Objectives and Risk Tolerance

If you have a large family, you may need a large car. Understanding your goals and objectives helps you make the right choices and select the right tools or investments for the job. Time, as well as your risk tolerance, can play an important part in picking the right investment. When and where to put your money are also important factors.

✦ If you need your money within 1 year, you want to keep it liquid. You may want to put it in a savings or money market account.

✦ If you need it between 1 to 5 years, find some safe vehicles such as CDs, GICs, Treasury Bills, or conservative bonds.

✦ If you need money in 5 years or later, consider stocks and bonds. The longer you invest the money, the more chance you may have to increase the amount of stock in your investment portfolio. Historically, statistics show that investors who kept their investment in stocks for 20 years did not suffer losses: Remember: Past performance does not guarantee future results.

Time in the market is far more important than timing the market.

ANNUAL RETURNS FOR S&P 500 INDEX USING ROLLING MONTHLY RETURNS BETWEEN 1950 AND 2010*

Holding pattern	Max. return	Avg. return	Min. return
1 year	53.4%	8.4%	-44.8%
3 years	30.1%	7.4%	-17.3%
5 years	26.2%	7.5%	-8.5%
10 years	16.8%	7.3%	-5.1%
20 years	14.4%	7.2%	2.4%

*Oppenheimer Asset Management Investment Strategy. http://usatoday30.usatoday.com money/perfi/stocks/2011-06-08-stocks-long-term-investing_n.htm

ASSET ALLOCATION:
Spreading Your Risk

Assume you have $10,000, and you want to invest for 20 years. You have several choices.

1. Play it safe. Put all of it in a CD that gives 3%. In 20 years, you'll have $18,061.

2. Divide the $10,000 into 5 slots. $2,000 is put into 5 different investments.

✦ Slot 1: You lost all of it. $0 left.

✦ Slot 2: You put it in a piggy bank. Since piggy gives no interest, you still have $2,000.

✦ Slot 3: You put it in a 2% savings account. You get $2,972.

✦ Slot 4: You invest in a bond fund and get 5% return. You'll have $5,307.

✦ Slot 5: You put it in stocks and earn 10%. You'll get $13,455.

Total of 5 slots ($23,733) versus the CD ($18,061).

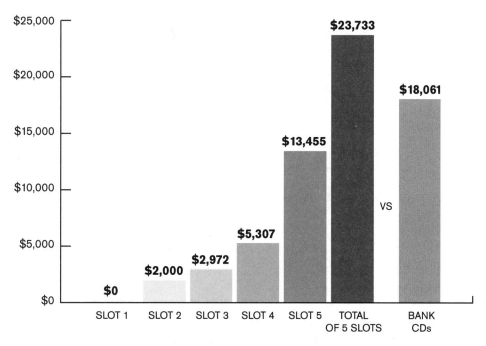

Please note that this is an example, not a suggestion to invest.

The above example gives you an idea about diversification. When some investments go bad, others may do better. Thus, you manage your risk for the long term by allocating your portfolio to suit your investment purpose.

Examples of Asset Allocation:

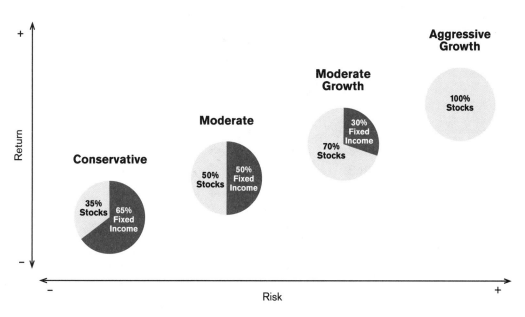

As your life changes, your purpose changes. When you're younger, you might be more willing to be aggressive. And when you're older, you may want to be less willing to take risks.*

*Asset allocation and diversification cannot assure a profit or guarantee against loss in declining markets. This is a hypothetical example for illustrative purposes only and is not intended to represent any specific investment. This example does not consider any costs associated with investing. Investments involve risk and you may incur a profit or a loss. (Source: Transamerica Asset Allocation Portfolios)

DOLLAR COST AVERAGING

A major concern of most investors is getting in the stock market at the wrong time.

Dollar Cost Averaging is a strategy to systematically purchase shares of a securities product to offset investment risk in a fluctuating market. This is a great discovery.

Put simply, you keep investing the same dollar amount every month to buy the same shares. If the share price goes up, you buy fewer shares. If the share price goes down, you buy more shares.

Example of $100 invested monthly:

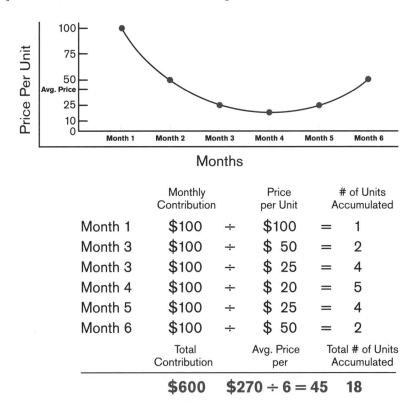

	Monthly Contribution		Price per Unit		# of Units Accumulated
Month 1	$100	÷	$100	=	1
Month 3	$100	÷	$ 50	=	2
Month 3	$100	÷	$ 25	=	4
Month 4	$100	÷	$ 20	=	5
Month 5	$100	÷	$ 25	=	4
Month 6	$100	÷	$ 50	=	2
	Total Contribution		Avg. Price per		Total # of Units Accumulated
	$600		**$270 ÷ 6 = 45**		**18**

Thus, in 6 months share prices go from $100 per share down to $20 per share and back to $50 per share, half of the original price. The total shares bought are 18 shares.

This hypothetical example shows that even when the share price goes down, you can receive a lower cost per share over time. The more shares you have, the better the result will be if the market goes back up.

Please be cautious. This is a mathematical model only. During a prolonged down market, if you get out at the low end, you'll lose money.*

Dollar cost averaging is a long-term strategy which does not assure a profit nor protect against a loss in a declining market. Investors should carefully consider their ability to continue regular purchases through periods of low price levels.

HOW RISKY IS THE RISK?

Understand the numbers game!

Average Rate of Return vs Actual Return

Example 1: A financial firm lists one of their products that earns a 10% average annual rate of return in the last 2 years based on this performance.

Year 1: +70%

Year 2: -50%

_____

20% in 2 years

10% average/year

Looking at this performance listing, you would think that you will make 10% a year. That sounds like a good deal.

However, the reality might shock you. If you invest $100, this is the result:

Year 1: $100 + 70% = $170

Year 2: $170 − 50% = $85

_____

Actual loss = $15   Isn't that amazing?!

In another example, say a product averaged 0% return over 2 years. You may think the investment stagnated and broke even.

Example 2: When you lose 50%, and you gain back 50%, you may think that your investment had no loss. But actually you do lose.

If you invest $100:

Year 1: -50% $100 − 50% = $50

Year 2: +50% $50 + 50% = $75

0% in 2 years

Example 3: So if you lose 50%, you must gain 100% just to break even.

Year 1: -50% $100 − 50% = $50

Year 2: +100% $50 + 100% = $100

This explains why many people today retired broke. After the dot.com and housing bubbles burst, the market fell -49% in 2000 and -56% in 2008. Even when the market bounced back, it was too late for many retirees!

HOW BIG IS THE SWING?

Some investments and stocks are very volatile. They rise very high and very quickly, but they can collapse just as fast. Others are more stable and fluctuate less.

Let's take a look at another mathematical example. Investment A fluctuates between +5% to +10%. But Investment B swings more wildly between -5% to +20%. Assume $100 investment.

Month	Investment A	Investment B
1	+10% = $110	+20% = $120
2	+5% = $115.50	-5% = $114
3	+10% = $127.05	+20% = $136.80
4	+5% = $133.40	-5% = $129.96
5	+10% = $146.74	+20% = $155.95
6	+5% = $154.08 total	-5% = $148.15 total
6 month avg	7.5%	7.5%

In this scenario, Investment A is doing better than B, even though both investments have the same 6-month average return. Keep in mind there are risk factors between investments that are more volatile and those more stable.*

This is a hypothetical example for illustrative purposes only and is not intended to represent any specific investment. This example does not consider any costs associated with investing. Investments involve risk and you may incur a profit or a loss.

DON'T BE TOO EMOTIONAL

"God created economists to make weather forecasters look good."
–Anonymous

The weather always does what it does best. It changes all the time.

What do we expect the stock market to do? The stock market does what it always does. It changes all the time, everyday. However, most people want to beat the stock market.

Although the weather changes, it's somewhat predictable. It gets cold in winter, warmer in spring, hot in summer, and cooler in fall.

You may not know how stocks change everyday, but in the last 100 years, they went up and down and up and down. But as it fluctuated over and over again, it has historically moved up over time.

The problem is most people want to know the short-term ups and downs, and they forget about long-term growth potential.

EMOTIONAL INVESTING OFTEN LEADS TO LOWER RETURNS

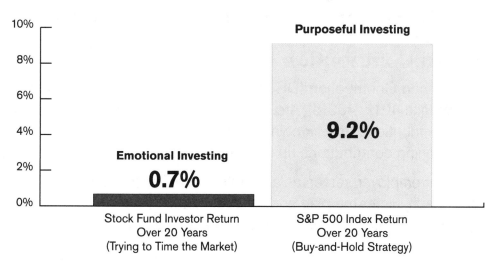

That's how many people lose money in the stock market. When they see it go up, most people enter the market without knowing that they are buying high. And when the market goes down, they panic and get out of the market, selling low. Unfortunately, many times when they get out, the stock may have hit bottom and begun to move up again.

Studies from Dalbar Inc. in the last 20 years show that investors who bought and sold in and out of the market based on their emotions had an average 0.7% annual return. During that same period, a "buy and hold" investment strategy in the S&P 500 Index averaged 9.2% annual return.*

Source: Quantitative Analysis of Investor Behavior, Copyright 2014, Dalbar, Inc.

RETIREMENT PLANS

Retirement plans fall into two basic categories: Defined Benefit Plan (DB) or Defined Contribution Plan (DC).

Defined Benefit Plan

Also known as a traditional pension, it pays a retiree a specific benefit based on years of service and salary level until they die. In some cases, the payout will continue for a spouse or a beneficiary.

Put simply, they're called Defined Benefit because you know what you're going to get when you retire.

This plan is quite costly for the employer. Most companies have dramatically scaled back on these plans or eliminated them altogether.

Defined Contribution Plan

Defined Contribution (DC) plans are normally known by their IRS Tax Code, like 401k, 403(b), etc. DC plans allow the employee to make pre-tax contributions to their own retirement account. Employers may make matching contributions up to a certain amount.

Your employer serves as a "plan sponsor" and has another company administer the plan and its investment. This plan administrator is typically a mutual fund company, a brokerage firm, or an insurance company.

You are responsible for the investment of your money by choosing investment options in the plan. Contribution limits are set every year to adjust to the high cost of living.

- ✦ **401k** is essentially a retirement savings account which offers tax advantages. It doesn't have the lifetime payout like pension plans.

- ✦ **403(b)** is similar to 401k but is available only for employees of tax-exempt organizations, like schools, hospitals, or religious organizations.

- ✦ **457** plans in general have similarities to 401k and are available to state and local public employees and to certain non-profit organizations.

Defined contribution plans invest with pre-tax contributions. Thus, withdrawing money before 59½ will be subject to early withdrawal penalties with some exceptions. And of course all distributions will be taxed as ordinary income.

These plans are called Defined Contribution because you know what you put in. But you won't know what you may get when you retire due to market fluctuations.

THE PASSIVE EMPLOYEE

Although 401ks and other DC plans are very popular, lack of understanding is still a major problem.

Many employees are passive participants. They contribute to their plans because people around them do so.

Few get involved enough or take the time to understand and monitor their plans. According to a recent AARP survey, 71% of people with 401ks didn't know they were paying fees for their retirement account. These fees can reduce their 401k balance by up to 30%.*

On top of that, without understanding the different investment options of the plan, they may pick the one that doesn't meet their risk tolerance and objectives. There are so many people who end up with poor results, and their retirement needs are not met.

*http://www.cnn.com/2012/06/27/opinion/hiltonsmith-retirement-savings

U.S. IRA AND ROTH IRA

Individual Retirement Account

Individual Retirement Account (IRA) is the most common form of retirement plan.*

Traditional IRAs have 2 major benefits.

✦ You do not pay tax on the money you contribute until you make a withdrawal.

✦ Any interest, dividend, or capital gains in the plan are tax-deferred until withdrawal.

Roth IRA

Roth IRAs are similar to traditional IRAs. However, the big difference is contributions are not tax deductible, and qualified distributions are tax free, provided you meet 2 guidelines:**

1. You leave the money in the account for at least 5 years after you make the first contribution.

2. You reach 59½, with exceptions for death or disability.

With Roth IRAs, you can leave money in the account for as long as you want.

Traditional IRAs don't allow that extension. You must start withdrawal by the time you reach age 70½.

Key Points to Remember

Traditional IRA: You don't pay tax on the money you put in, but you pay tax when you take it out.

Roth IRA: You pay tax on the money when you put it in, but you don't pay tax when you take it out, assuming you meet the criteria defined above.

IRAs and Roth IRAs have limits on how much you can contribute each year, and you may face penalties if you withdraw before the designated retirement age.

IRA Rollovers

IRA rollovers are an important feature to move your money to a better investment account of your choice. Unfortunately, there are many people who do not use it for its full potential. Not only can you rollover one IRA into another, you can rollover 401ks, 403(b)s, and the like into an IRA or Roth IRA.

Distributions from IRAs are taxable as ordinary income. For any withdrawals prior to age 59½, a 10% federal penalty tax may apply to the taxable amount. Contributions may be tax deductible depending on income limits.
**Earnings in a Roth IRA grow tax-deferred. Contributions are made with after-tax money. Non-qualified distributions of earnings are taxed as ordinary income and prior to age 59½, a 10% federal penalty tax may apply to the taxable amount. Eligibility to participate depends on adjustable gross income amounts.

SIMPLE IRA

Savings Incentive Match Plan for Employees (SIMPLE) is a type of traditional IRA for small businesses and self-employed people. Contributions are tax deductible. Investments have the potential to grow tax deferred until withdrawal.

Employers are required to match contribution with employees up to 3% of salary or 2% flat of pay whether the employee contributes or not.

SEP IRA

Simplified Employee Pension (SEP) is a retirement plan set up by the employer, including the self-employed person. The employer makes tax-deductible contributions for the employee, including the business owner.

Employees can't contribute; only the employer can. Employees don't pay tax until withdrawal.

Just like other IRA plans, 59½ and 70½ rules apply. Withdrawals before 59½ receive a penalty with certain exceptions, such as medical or education expenses or first-time home purchasing.

Both SIMPLE and SEP IRAs are simple and low cost to set up.

COLLEGE/UNIVERSITY SAVINGS PLANS

When having children, parents don't often think about how much their kids will cost them. However, it takes a lot of money to raise a child. According to the U.S. Department of Agriculture, in 2013 it will cost a middle-income couple $245,000 to raise a child until 18 years old.[*] And this does not include college costs. The cost for Canada is $243,660.[**] That's roughly $1,000 per month from birth to adulthood.

But the big bill comes when your child goes to college.[***]

TYPE OF TUITION	4-YEAR TUITION 2013	TUITION & FEES IN 18 YEARS: 2031
Private	$129,700	$312,200
Public	$38,300	$92,200

Canadian universities are lower at $6,348 for the year 2012-13[****]

Where do you get the money for your child to go to the college of their choice?

Looking back, you may remember all the toys, parties, and trips you spent on your children over the last 18 years. You took care of them so well, except you didn't prepare for the high cost of education.

What if you thought ahead, cut down some unnecessary expenses, and put those savings into an account. You might have had a brighter scenario.

Many parents end up having to withdraw money out of their pension or retirement account. Some borrow against their cash value in a life insurance policy. Others get loans from equity in their house and go into debt. Some have a 529 plan.

*http://money.cnn.com/2014/08/18/pf/child-cost
**http://www.canadianliving.com/life/money/how_much_does_it_cost_to_raise_kids_in_canada.php
***The College Board (www.savingforcollege.com)
****http://www.cbc.ca/news/canada/university-tuition-rising-to-record-levels-in-canada-1.1699103

U.S. 529 Savings Plan

With a 529 savings plan, parents open an account and choose an investment strategy. The money you put in is after tax. Potential earnings accumulate tax free, and withdrawals can be made tax free when it's time to pay for college expenses, such as tuition, books, room and board.

529 is a state-sponsored college savings plan but open to nonresidents. Thus, parents can shop around for the best plan to meet their financial goals and needs.

However, if your kid decides not to go to college, you can transfer the money to another family member for college. If all your children decide to skip school and become rock stars, then the money is subject to regular income taxes plus a 10% penalty on gains.

Please note that 529 plans affect a family's eligibility for financial aid because it is considered an asset.*

*While investing in college savings plans allows for the opportunity for growth, they do come with risk. You may lose money, or it may not grow enough to pay for college since the rate of return and principal value of the underlying investments will fluctuate. Also, unlike prepaid tuition plans, they don't lock in tuition prices. There are various fees and expenses associated with 529's which vary among plans. You should review the offering document carefully for complete details.

Canadian Education: RESP

In Canada, the Registered Education Savings Plan (RESP) is a way for parents and grandparents to help save for a child's education. For rules concerning RESP, see: *http://www.cra-arc.gc.ca/tx/ndvdls/tpcs/ resp-reee/menu-eng.html.*

REGISTERED RETIREMENT SAVINGS PLAN

(Tax Deductible and Tax Deferred)

A Registered Retirement Savings Plan (RRSP) is a savings vehicle for Canadians to save for their retirement. Inside an RRSP you have many options for investing.

All contributions are tax deductible. For example, if you are in a 40% tax bracket, you would save $4,000 in taxes on a $10,000 contribution. Your net cost of the $10,000 is only $6,000.

All the growth inside the RRSP grows tax deferred until withdrawal. This can have a good effect on the value of the RRSP since no tax is paid on any growth along the way. But remember: The tax will be paid later when you withdraw.

Anyone who has earned income, has a social insurance number, and filed a tax return can contribute to an RRSP up till the year they turn 71. At this age, the RRSP holder has 3 options: 1) take the accumulated money and pay all of the tax, 2) convert the RRSP into an annuity, or 3) convert the RRSP into a Registered Retirement Income Fund (RRIF) that pays out a minimum amount of income every year.

TAX FREE SAVINGS ACCOUNT
(Tax Free Distributions)

A Tax Free Savings Account (TFSA) is a savings vehicle for Canadians to save inside their own tax shelter. You have different investment choices. The beauty of TFSA is that regardless of how much growth you have inside your account, you will never have to pay tax.

It is by far the most tax advantageous vehicle available to Canadians. This plan is very similar to Roth IRA in the U.S.

RRSP OR TFSA?

This is an ongoing debate. Which is better to contribute to: an RRSP or a TFSA?

Most Canadians should be using RRSPs to save for their retirement if it makes sense. But RRSPs do not necessarily make sense for all Canadians. This is why it's important to reach out to a professional to help advise you on your personal situation. If you're serious about your financial future and if it makes sense for your individual tax situation, you should consider contributing to both an RRSP and a TFSA.

SOCIAL SECURITY

Congress established the Social Security Act of 1935 to help supplement the incomes of retirees. Unfortunately, Social Security (SS) has become the only source of income for millions of Americans.

Social Security is funded by current payroll taxes (FICA) from you and your employer. Thus, the shrinking pool of workers per retiree will be a big challenge to the system. The following chart lists the full retirement age by year of birth.*

AGE TO RECEIVE FULL SOCIAL SECURITY BENEFITS

Year of birth	Full retirement age
1943-1954	66
1955	66 and 2 months
1956	66 and 4 months
1957	66 and 6 months
1958	66 and 8 months
1959	66 and 10 months
1960 and later	67

Note: People who were born on January 1 of any year should refer to the previous year.

You can start receiving benefits as early as age 62, or you can wait until full retirement age. Of course, early retirement will give you fewer benefits.

Your spouse can also receive half of your benefit amount whether he or she works or not.

*http://www.ssa.gov/retire2/retirechart.htm

TAXES ON YOUR SOCIAL SECURITY BENEFIT

Your SS benefits will be taxed depending on your other incomes:

+ if you're still working, your salary;

+ if you're earning interest and capital gains;

+ if you're withdrawing from retirement savings such as IRA, 401k, 403(b), and other employer-sponsored programs;

+ if you're earning gains from annuities distributions.

However, Roth IRA distributions are income-tax free, assuming certain requirements are met as outlined previously. Withdrawals and loans from insurance policies are also not a taxable event and thus won't be counted.

Depending on your income, combined income from you and your spouse will be subject to tax.

Thus, Uncle Sam will be there even after you retire.

So, will your tax rate be lower when you retire? It depends.

Chances are if you have good income and make sizeable withdrawals from pensions and qualified plans, in addition to your SS benefits, you may still be in a high tax bracket.

Furthermore, your mortgage is most likely paid off, so there is no mortgage deduction. The kids are grown up, so no dependents deduction or kids tax credits can be claimed either.

Worse, if you fail to do Required Minimum Distributions (RMD) at age 70½, you will have to pay 50% of tax penalties on top of the income tax on the RMD amount.

MANAGED GROWTH

How do you win the money game?

If money were a game, many of us would be losing. Making big income does not necessarily mean that you are going to win.

Millions are drowning in a sea of debt. Bankruptcies don't just happen to the working poor. It befalls people from all walks of life. Some people make a lot, but they may spend a lot too. Others make big bets when the market is hot but shy away when the market is undervalued.

They lose and don't know why they lose. And those who win don't often know why they win. If they knew, they would continue to do what makes them win and avoid what makes them lose.

Lack of knowing how money works is the main cause for losing the money game.

GROWTH OR SAFETY?

Do you want growth or safety?

When thinking about safety for their money, most people think about banks. When they want growth, most think about investment securities.

The problem is that if you want growth, you may not get safety. And if you want safety, you may not get the growth to beat inflation. Sound like a catch-22?

Can you get both growth potential and safety? It can be possible.

When you play sports, you have to play both offense and defense. You've got to be strong on both sides. You can't have all the players attack and leave no one to defend the home base.

Thus, you have to diversify. You allocate your assets into different positions. You use dollar cost averaging to capitalize on the downtime in the market.

Occasionally, you rebalance your investment mix if your objectives have changed and to make sure your investments are doing what you need them to do.

Take advantage of tax advantages allowed by law to grow more and keep more. A tax savings of 20% is as good as a 20% gain in rate of return.

And you must definitely have a good defense with protection of your life, your investment, and your estate.

When building your future and making financial decisions, you should ask these questions.

1. Can it potentially grow to achieve my goal?
2. Is it safe enough?
3. Does it have tax advantages?
4. Does it have proper protection?

If you have a good answer to each of these questions, you are likely moving in the right direction toward your goal. Growth is good, but managed growth is better.

FORMULA 10/20

Knowing What You Need

A recent article in the *Financial Analysts Journal* suggests that Americans need to save more—not just a little more, but vastly more.*

To be assured of having enough money for a comfortable retirement, they advise you to have a total of 22 times your income by the time you retire. Thus, if you make $50,000 per year, the target retirement number should be $1,100,000.

Many people today will live long lives, some to the age of 100. The need may be much bigger than normally thought.

To simplify things, you can round down 22 to 20 times your annual income for your retirement.

As for protecting your family, many financial professionals normally suggest 10 times your annual income in order to meet the insurance need for your family.

For example, if you make $50,000 a year, then your life insurance need would be $500,000. This amount of money would allow the surviving spouse to take care of the children for the next 10 years or more, giving him or her enough time to make the transition.

So if you die too soon, you'll need 10 times your income.

And if you live too long, you'll need 20 times your income.

Hence, the formula 10/20.

Please keep in mind that this is simply a suggestive "rule of thumb". It's does not by any means replace the actual need of the individual in protection or retirement. However, for those who want a simple solution, this 10/20 formula can be a handy tool.

http://blogs.wsj.com/moneybeat/2014/01/31/retiring-on-your-own-terms

MEDICARE

Medicare is your health insurance after the age of 65 in the U.S. Unless you are still covered by your employer's health plan, you must enroll in Medicare before you can get additional private Medicare supplement coverage.

Medicare Has 4 Parts: A, B, C, and D.

Part A is medical insurance for hospital visits and is free for most people.

Part B is medical insurance for doctor visits and other health care providers and is not free. Current monthly premiums are $104.90 in 2014 or higher if you're wealthy.

Part C: See below.

Part D is insurance for drug coverage to help lower drug costs.

Enrollment in Part A & B through the Social Security Administration

There are 2 enrollment periods.

+ Initial enrollment period: You have a total of 7 months, 3 months before and 3 months after your birthday month.

+ Special enrollment period: For people with employer coverage, you can do the initial sign up right away or within 7 months after your group coverage ends.

If not, you still can enroll during the General Enrollment period, January 1 to March 31 of each year. Late enrollment penalties will be assessed.

After signing up with Part A & B, you can sign up with Part D.

Medicare Supplement (Medigap)

This is the insurance plan you buy to pay for the "gap" that Medicare does not cover such as deductibles, copays, and coinsurances.

Benefits are standardized among all the plans. So whether you buy from Mutual of Omaha, Blue Cross, or AARP, the benefits are the same. Thus, it's important to find a cost-effective plan that could save you money.

Part C: Medicare Advantage

This part includes all the benefits and services covered under Part A & B. It also usually includes Part D.

Part C is an alternative to the original Medicare. Insurers for Part C receive a per capita amount from Medicare to provide this coverage.

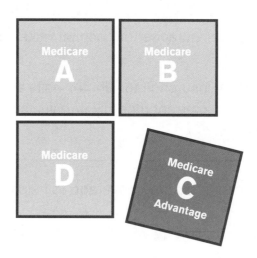

Put simply, if you want an HMO like Kaiser, you will go to participating doctors and hospitals of their plan in their network. In this case, you would choose Medicare Advantage (Part C), which is usually cheaper and sometimes no cost.

But if you want to go to the doctors, specialists, and hospitals of your choice, you are better off with a regular Medicare supplement, and you must pay more.

To make it simple:
- ✦ **If you think about Medicare, you think PPO.**
- ✦ **If you think about Medicare Advantage, you think HMO.**

Every year, from October 15 to December 7, you can change your plan during this Annual Election Period if necessary to fit with your health care needs.

Due to the high cost of health care in the U.S., it's a big concern to both the government and our senior citizens.

LONG TERM CARE

Long term care (LTC) is a growing problem that families have to deal with. And with growing numbers of retirees, the problem is only getting worse.

Think about it. If you have to take care of the parents while having a job and a family, it can be a huge burden. Many people may have to quit their job to look after their parents. Even elderly persons who lack money and assistance have to take care of their spouses, and they are not physically or mentally capable to handle it.

LTC is one of the major types of protection in planning for your future or for your aging parents. For most of us, LTC is not an issue of "what if" it will happen but rather *when* it will happen. The sooner you have this protection, the better because you never know when something will happen.

Who needs long term care? There is a good chance you do.

+ 70% of people over age 65 will require some LTC services.[*]

+ 40% of those receiving LTC are between 18 and 64.[**]

The cost of LTC is astounding. The average annual cost of a nursing home is $83,580 in the U.S. and $47,000 in Canada.[***,****]

The cost is lower when you are younger.

Health insurance or Medicare can help pay the cost of immediate medical expenses but not for the long term care of chronically ill people.

LTC pays for the insured who becomes chronically ill, which is defined as the inability to perform at least two of the following activities: bathing, continence, dressing, eating, toileting, and transferring.

You can purchase LTC as a stand-alone policy, or you can buy it as a rider in an insurance policy.

Take care of your LTC because you won't want to be a burden to your loved ones.

*http://www.longermcare.gov/LTC/Main_Site/index.aspx (June 2012)
**http://www.longtermcare.gov/LTC/Main_Site/Paying/Costs/Index.aspx (June 2012)
***Sources: Statistics Canada, CANSIM table 202-0407. Financial Post. (2012). Long term care takes planning.
****http://business.financialpost.com/2012/10/17/long-term-care-takes-planning

ESTATE PLANNING

Few people think about estate planning. Of course, if people don't do much in terms of savings, investment, and insurance, estate planning will not be on their priority list.

Most think estate planning is for rich people who live in mansions high up on a hill. But in fact, everyone has an estate. Your estate is everything you own minus your debt, such as your house, car, money in the bank, family heirlooms, etc.

Imagine you worked hard your entire life and built up an estate. You want to pass it on to someone, but it ends up with someone else due to your lack of planning.

Thus, a Will or Trust is a tool for you to organize how you want your estate distributed when you pass away.

WILLS

A will is a legal document that allows you to distribute your property to those of your choosing. It allows you to assign specific items from your estate to one person and other items to other people or an organization. You can also name an Executor, the person who will carry out your wishes.

Wills also give you the opportunity to pick a guardian for your young children. The guardian will be responsible for their welfare.

If you don't have a will, the government will use their standard will to decide how to distribute your estate, and you may not like what they do.

TRUSTS

A will only takes effect after you die. However, a living trust can benefit you while you are still alive. Living trusts are generally revocable, which means you can always make changes to them.

With a living trust, all your assets like your home, bank account, stocks, and bonds are put into a trust, administered for your benefit during your lifetime, and then transferred to your beneficiary when you die.

Most people name themselves as the trustee in charge of managing these assets. Thus, you have control over it. You can also name a successor trustee in case you are unable to manage the trust.

So having a trust is like you creating a corporation where you put all your assets in it, and you run it or have someone run it for you.

Living trusts may cost more to prepare, fund, or manage than a will. Having one helps to avoid probate costs for all the assets in the trust.

Thus, you should have a will or a living trust to take care of your family, or else the government will do it.

Proper planning with professional help can be very important for you to leave a legacy and preserve your estate for the causes you worked all your life for.

SAVING YOUR FUTURE

A Plan of Action

You can make the change. You can take charge of your future. One of the greatest miracles in life is that you can change your life by simply changing your mind.

A common secret shared among highly successful people is the way they think. They think and grow rich. Many of them come from the same place that you are from, and they made it big.

If you want to make a change, you must know whether you have a problem, and then it needs to be addressed. No one knows it better than you and your family. And you must have the courage to acknowledge it and change it.

Spend Less, Make More

There is no magic for building a solid financial foundation. Just like there is no magic in losing weight, you simply eat right and exercise more. That will triumph over any special diet or pill. Likewise, no financial professional can help a person who spends more than he or she earns.

You can make more money. The old way of thinking—getting a good job, working until 65 and retiring happily—is over. Nowadays you should be more proactive in your thinking about making money.

Whether you stay a few more hours overtime, get a second job, work part time, or freelance, you can use your special skills and know-how to make money. Many successful stories in business came from things people started in their garage or from their favorite hobbies. If you look for it, you'll find it.

Make it a mission to change your family's future.

1. Increase your cash flow. Make more money when you can, while you can. Have multiple sources of income.

2. Spend less. Cut down your expenses. It's not how much you earn that counts. It's what you keep. Set aside 5, 10, 15% of your income to savings.

3. Reduce your debt and liabilities. Interest on the debt will interfere with your goal for long-term asset accumulation.

4. Understand how money works. You must take time to understand how money works. You must learn how to make money work for you.

5. Have a financial goal. Set up a plan of action.

✦ **Take care of your responsibility**. Have proper protection.

✦ **Build up your wealth**. Start to save. It's not how much. It's how disciplined you are to save. Start with a small amount and increase it gradually.

6. Embrace change and expect to succeed.

✦ Change your habits.

Not only can you change the way you think, you must also change your habits. Two things that can make great changes to your life are the books you read and the people you meet.

The more you spend time with the wrong crowd, you probably won't be right. If you want to be successful, move to a better environment. Be around successful people. If you know how to tell your kids not to hang around a certain crowd, you know how to do it too.

A better environment will help provide better thinking and better solutions.

✦ Expect to succeed.

You don't win or lose overnight. You win or lose by degree. If you want to win, make your way back toward winning, step by step, and follow through to completion. Expect to succeed.

✦ Get out of your cocoon.

See the world. There are people who are better off than you, but there are a lot more who are even more worse off.

You are special. You know you are somebody. And you can do a lot of great things. You're the head of the family. You're the captain of your ship. Set sail, feel the wind, enjoy the journey.

SOME FOOD FOR THOUGHT

Did you know that half the world—over 3 billion people—live on less than $2.50 a day?

And at least 80% of humanity lives on less than $10 a day.

According to UNICEF, 22,000 children die each day due to poverty.

Nearly 1 billion people enter the 21st century unable to read a book or sign their names.

In 1960, 20% of people in the world's richest countries had 30 times the income of the poorest 20%; in 1997, 74 times as much.

In 2005, the world's wealthiest 20% accounted for 76.6% of total private consumption; the poorest fifth just 1.5%.

And some numbers on our priorities:*

RICH COUNTRIES' SPENDING PRIORITY		ADDITIONAL COST FOR BASIC NEEDS IN POOR COUNTRIES	
	$US Billions		$US Billions
Cosmetics in U.S.	8	Basic Education for All	6
Perfume U.S. & Europe	12	Water and Sanitation	9
Pet food U.S. & Europe	17	Reproductive Health for Women	12
Cigarettes in Europe	50	Basic Health/Nutrition	13

Richer or poorer, it's up to where you live and how you think.

Hopefully, even as poor as you think you are now, you may be richer than billions of people in the world, and you still can save and spare a few bucks to help the many people out there who are much less fortunate than you.

*http://www.globalissues.org/article/26/poverty-facts-and-stats